CYCLING EUROPE

GREAT DAY RIDES

Also by Michael J. Lyon

Cycling Along Europe's Rivers:
Bicycle Touring Made Easy and Affordable

CYCLING EUROPE

GREAT DAY RIDES

OVER 90 BEAUTIFUL DAY RIDES
FROM 30 FANTASTIC EUROPEAN CITIES

MICHAEL J. LYON

CYCLE TOURING BOOKS

Text © 2021 by Michael J. Lyon
Photos © 2021 by Michael J. Lyon, Joshua Lyon, Michael Polacek

Cover Photo: Entering Chambord by Tom Morrow
Layout Design: Davor Nikolic
Maps: Michael J. Lyon with © Printmaps.net

Published By:
Cycle Touring Books
www.cycletouringbooks.com

ISBN: 978-0-578-74054-6

To my wife Kusavadee for understanding why I love these rides; to my riding son and riding partner Joshua; to my Uncle Harvey, who introduced me to cycle touring and rode with me until the age of 87; and to my parents who made everything possible.

TABLE OF CONTENTS

LIST OF MAPS

INTRODUCTION

We left our hotel in the historic center of the French town of Blois, taking a short ride past the Chateau Royal de Blois, then across the old Le Pont Jacques Gabriel bridge spanning the Loire River, and headed northeast along the bike path following the river. Several kilometers down the bike path we turned away from the river toward the magnificent Chambord Chateau. The ride was easy on our rented bikes given that we were carrying only day bags; one of my friends had it even easier by having rented an e-bike. There it was -- Chambord -- arguably the grandest chateau on the Loire. We rolled up the formal driveway originally designed for horse and carriage, but now perfect for approaching by bike -- and far removed from the tour buses that approach in packs by road. We were only adding a few days of cycling to our multifaceted European vacation, taking a short train ride from Paris to our riding base hotel in Blois -- but these few easy days riding near the Loire River with our rented bikes and no hassles were my favorite days of the trip!

This book is dedicated to this type of cycling -- amazing day rides in Europe that can be added to a general European holiday.

Every summer over almost thirty years I have enjoyed a couple weeks of self-guided cycling tours following bike paths along Europe's grand rivers. In 2013, I wrote a book focused on this type of longer cycle touring: *Cycling Along Europe's Rivers: Bicycle Touring Made Easy and Affordable*. I am pleased that so many readers and riders enjoyed this book and found useful information for planning various longer rides in Europe.

Unlike my first book, which presented point-to-point, extended, self-contained, cycle touring options -- where riders carried all their gear and moved hotels every night or two -- this book is designed for riders to stay in one base hotel for multiple nights and enjoy one to four day rides using locally rented bikes. With these types of shorter rides, cycling can be added to a general European vacation without disrupting your general trip itinerary and involving minimal additional logistic complications or luggage -- perfect if you don't have the time, interest, or travelling companion well-suited to a longer biking tour.

Over my decades of touring I identified certain major tourist cities especially well-suited for these short ride opportunities beyond the city rides offered almost everywhere these days. Each of these cities provide access to rides that are easy to navigate, generally flat, and interesting. These major cities include Munich, Frankfurt, Hamburg, Prague, Vienna, Bratislava, Budapest, Paris, Florence, and Venice.

I also discovered smaller cities and lakes, some less well known, that provide fantastic bases for multiple interesting day rides. Some of these cities and lakes included in this book are Passau, Trier, Nantes, Blois, Verona, Padua, Lake Balaton, and Lake Bodensee.

For some cities, towns, or lakes, I suggest one- or two-day rides, and in others I suggest up to four days of riding if you have the time. Two or three base locations can be combined to make for a longer cycling adventure. For example, providing up to twelve days of day rides, with only one or two hotel moves. In many cases, these different bases might only be one to two hours apart by train.

This book does not present an exhaustive list of day rides from a location nor is it meant to replace a general travel guide or detailed map, such as the *Bikeline* map books. It is meant to give you an idea of where to go, what to expect, and how to plan.

I have tried to organize this book to provide the practical information you need:

- 30 suggested cities to stay in while enjoying day riding.
- Ride suggestions and highlights from each city (over 90 day rides in all).
- Basic navigation tips that are not detailed turn-by-turn directions, but do point out important waypoints, interesting stops, and general guidance, given that these routes are generally relatively straightforward and well-marked.
- Information on how to get from one place to another with your bike when not riding -- such as how to use trains or sightseeing boats to return to your hotel after one-way longer rides.
- Bike rental information.
- Hotels suggestions.
- Suggested maps and books, including the *Esterbauer* Bikeline guidebooks.

Many of the suggested rides involve riding along Europe's rivers, which often have well-developed and marked bike trails. European civilization generally developed along these rivers, so river rides provide the opportunity to visit many fascinating cities (both large and small), castles, monasteries, vineyards, museums, and fortresses. Distances between stops are relatively short because these river towns developed when travel was slower, which means that towns formed closer together.

Some Caveats:

- **Some Overlap with the First Book**: I appreciate that many thousands of cyclists have purchased my book, *"Cycling Along Europe's Rivers."* There will be some redundancies between these two books since I intend this book to be a stand-alone guide, so I apologize to readers if I repeat myself from time-to-time.
- **Non-Exhaustive Route List**: This book presents many suggested rides, but unquestionably there are many additional options not covered here. This is a sample of rides I have done, but not an exhaustive list. Improvise, and let me know additional ideas for the next edition!

- **One-Way Train Facilitated Rides**: I often recommend point-to-point rides, with a train or boat planned for the return to your base city. This type of travel is easy to do in Europe and these trains rides are often an hour or less. Shorter rides are also available by taking a train back from a closer target city, or riding shorter round-trip loops without going all the way to the end point of a route.
- **General Travel Guide Suggested**: I make some suggestions for hotels and other attractions, but in order to keep this book to a reasonable length, this is far from an exhaustive list. I recommend having a general travel guide or app for more detailed information on each attraction along a route.

Finally, I wanted to mention that I wrote much of this book during the pandemic shutdown of 2020, when, for the first time since 1994, I could not ride in Europe. In some ways, writing this book kept me connected with riding in Europe and made my future rides all the more anticipated.

I hope you enjoy the book and it inspires you to add an additional cycling dimension to your travels!

PART ONE

OVERVIEW

Why Take Day-Riding Adventures in Europe?

So, you are going to Europe on vacation, don't have the time or interest for a longer dedicated cycle tour, but are looking for some easy to organize riding beyond the standard city cycling tours. This book is designed for you!

It is clearly worth considering adding interesting, short day rides to your trip both as an added dimension to your vacation and as the opportunity to gain experience that might lead to a longer cycle tour in the future.

Riding along Europe's bike trails offers special advantages:
- Get away from the crowds of major cities to locations less visited and sometimes not even in the guidebooks.
- Well-developed and marked bike trails allow riders to stay away from traffic even when riding from city to city.
- Historic sites such as old churches and castles, and not just the ones that everyone always talks about.
- Relatively short distances between sites and cities given that Europe's historic cities developed before faster transportation and are situated closer together.
- Reasonable hotel accommodations that provide basic but clean facilities.
- Great food, beer, and wine means that eating local cuisine and drink is one of the added pleasures of European cycling.

Riding Europe's Rivers: Cycle Touring Made Easy

Riding anywhere in Europe is terrific, but one of the best ways to cycle in Europe is along the extensive river bike trail network.

While some of the rides in this book take you away from rivers on bike trails or quieter roads, most of the rides take advantage of an amazing network of bike trails along many of Europe's rivers. Development along Europe's rivers preceded other forms of transportation, such as rail or highway transportation, which means that even today many European rivers are navigable and inter-connected, and continue to play critical roles in transportation, shipping, commerce, and tourism. They often support convenient logistic infrastructure and interesting sites.

One of the most important advantages of riding along rivers is that the routes are **generally flat.** This is a critical element for making these rides easy and accessible to riders of various abilities. I try and point out where the suggested rides involve more hills.

Here is a summary of some of the additional reasons we like to tour along Europe's rivers:

- Great, safe, riding. Most river bike trails are paved and without car traffic, though some sections might be unpaved, and others might involve riding on smaller roads.
- Easy navigation, with the river itself serving as the ultimate visual guide.
- Good logistics given that rail lines often run along rivers, providing easy access to our "sag" support system.
- Many rivers have sightseeing boats that follow the cycling routes. These boats usually allow bikers aboard, providing a great way to take a break for lunch (while cruising) and skip a section of the ride. These boats also often travel through some of the most scenic parts of a river, providing a relaxing way to experience the river's beauty and sites from a different perspective than possible from a bike.

- Many towns, both small and large, are located along the route. Many of Europe's most interesting cities are along rivers. Rivers also served as trading routes, leaving a prosperous, interesting historic and architectural legacy.
- Rivers can pass through gorges, providing stunning views of the natural surroundings as well as of castles, monasteries, and vineyards along the side hills.
- River valleys often support amazing wine vineyards, providing a great opportunity to experience many different local European wines and even visits to various wineries.

Typical Bike Path Along River

PREPARING FOR DAY RIDES

Riding for Everyone

Day rides can be enjoyed by almost everyone, and require little training or preparation. Suggested day rides are 32 km to 80 km, and, depending on your level and interest, are available to riders across the spectrum of ages and abilities. Almost all rides can be shortened by ending early and taking a train back, or by riding shorter roundtrip loops. With the growing availability of e-bikes -- there is no excuse not to take a ride!

- **All Ages**: Age 1-90+. I took multiweek annual tours with my uncle until he was 87, and did them all without an e-bike!
- **All Abilities**: Novice through expert riders can enjoy these day rides. The introduction of e-bikes makes it especially easy for riders of different abilities to ride together.
- **Groups**: Riders of different levels can tour together, using e-bikes, touring boats, or trains to skip sections of a day's ride and still meet at the final destination.
- **Kids**: These rides are well-suited to riding with kids and families given that most are on bike paths, with no or little traffic. These routes also provide fun and interesting stops for kids -- and multiple opportunities for amazing ice cream stops! Younger kids can ride in trailers behind parents (these can often be rented), though I think that there is a limit to how far you can go in a day with this method and keep your kids (and yourself) from going crazy. If pulling a trailer, I would recommend planning for no more than maybe 40 km per day.
- **Non-Riders**: Non-riders can participate by staying at the same base hotel and city as their riding companions and can consider a sightseeing boat or train ride meeting their companion along the route. But even the most committed non-rider should consider an e-bike rental; this option allows even less-experienced companions to join for shorter excursions.

How to Prepare

Preparing for these day rides is not complicated or time-consuming. Here are some pre-trip tips:

- **Minimal Training**: If possible, do some riding before the trip. Even a few 32 km to 40 km rides during the weeks before the trip can help.
- **Route Selection and Reservations**: If feasible, pre-select the base location for your trip so that you can make necessary hotel and bike rental reservations.
- **Travel Guidebooks/Travel Apps**: Collect information about the route, preferably in digital format (Kindle versions, for example) that can be viewed on your phone and support your itinerary. The Trip Advisor app can be useful, as well as digital versions of Rick Steve's or Frommer's travel guides.
- **Route Maps**: It is not required to have a dedicated route map book for these rides since most routes are well-marked and relatively easy to navigate, but more on this topic under the Navigation section of this book.
- **Checklist**: Consider the checklist at the end of this book for suggestions on preparing for your trip.

What to Pack

Pack as few extra items as you can to support your day riding, both in your general luggage, and during rides on your bike. Contact your targeted bike rental shop to determine what they will provide or rent. Don't plan to take more on your rides than can fit easily in a reasonably sized day-riding pack, with the potential of an additional handlebar bag in case you really need more space.

- **Generally available with a rented bike:**
  - Bike pump (small).
  - Tire changing tool and optional chain repair tool (sometimes available).
  - Extra tube or repair kit.
  - One lock per bike.
  - Day pack (often provided at an additional cost, so consider bringing your own).
  - Helmet, usually available for a small fee, or bring your own if you want higher quality, better fitting helmet.

- **Pack the following from home and bring with you on your rides:**
  - GPS (optional) and a compass.
  - Multicomponent tool (screwdriver, hex wrenches); these are sometimes available with rental, so verify ahead.
  - Small first-aid kit, including Band-Aids, Benadryl for bites, and triple antibiotic cream.
  - Phone that is international-call capable.
  - Suntan lotion.
  - Riding gloves.
  - Raincoat.
  - Potentially bring your own cycling shoes and even pedals, especially if you prefer clipless pedals.

What to Wear and Bring

You don't need to bring much extra gear on your trip for these rides. Even one set of riding gear might be enough if you don't mind washing clothes in the sink during the evening (as we do) and taking advantage of the hotel's hair dryer when needed.

Note on packing gear: I use large zip-lock plastic bags with sliding locks for packing my riding gear. They are low cost, waterproof, and when air is pressed out, very space efficient. You can also use these bags to pack items in your day riding bags for protection and space efficiency.

The following is a suggestion for the minimum clothing to bring on a trip. If you have more space in your luggage, consider bringing a bit more:

- One riding shirt. A standard drip-dry shirt that you use on your general trip will work, though I prefer bright-color cycle shirts for extra safety and comfort.
- One pair of riding shorts, which definitely make the ride more comfortable. Alternatively, consider padded cycle underwear that can be used with general travel shorts.
- One pair of riding shoes. Most rental bikes do not have clipless pedals, but you can bring your own pedals. Normal athletic shoes are also fine, just a bit less efficient.
- One lightweight raincoat (such as made with GORE-TEX), with vents, just in case of rain. This is also useful for your general European touring.
- A pair of lightweight cycle socks are always useful.

Bike Rental

For longer cycle trips I always bring my own bike, but over the almost thirty years I have been touring I have seen great improvement in the quality and availability of bike rentals. For the day riding discussed in this book, renting a bike makes perfect sense. The type of bike you select depends on the routes you are riding (road, paved trail, or unpaved) and what you the most comfortable riding.

Finding a bike shop that rents the type of bike you want is an important consideration for each base city and route selection. I note at least one rental shop in each base location. I also try and note if a listed rental shop has a large bike selection, but I encourage you to email or call ahead to confirm availability and reserve the bike and style you want.

I don't recommend the bike-share bikes, if you have a choice. These bikes are generally not as well maintained as standard bike shop rentals or generally well-suited for the longer rides suggested in this book.

The most common types of bikes you will have to choose from include:

- **Road Bikes:** I am not a fan of standard road bikes for longer touring because I have found that they are not tough enough for these trips, especially when weighted down. I generally like wider, more flexible, and safer tires even if I sacrifice some speed. However, if you like road bikes, they should be fine for most of these day rides, so long as the route is generally paved and in good condition.

- **European Standard Hybrids:** Most rental locations in Europe feature relatively heavy, sturdy, hybrid-style bikes, often without shocks. I would suggest renting the highest quality bike available in the shop, which tend to be lighter and with more gears. Consider a bike with a lockable front shock, if they have one in stock.

- **E-bikes:** E-bikes are now everywhere on European bike paths and are designed for all types of riders. I have seen extremely fit young riders zoom by on high-end e-bike mountain bikes. These types of bikes certainly deserve serious consideration for a trip, and are increasingly available in rental locations. Charging stations are becoming more common in hotels and along the pathways.

These are additional rental considerations:

- **Rental Budget:** The cost of rentals will vary, but here are some general rates to expect (2020 rates), with the ranges shown being arranged from basic rental to higher-end rental to expensive e-bike: These are additional rental considerations:
  - **Single-Day Rental:** €16 - €24 - €40.
  - **Two-Day Rental:** €30- €45 -€75.
  - **Three-Day Rental:** €40 – €60 – €110.

- **Standard Equipment:** Rental bikes often come with pumps, repair kits, spare tubes, rear racks, and locks.

- **Extras:** Extra items can often be rented for an added charge. Check on availability before your trip since this might dictate what you bring with you:

- ○ **Helmet:** €2 per day.
- ○ **Trailer Bike:** (for traveling with kids) €8 per day.
- ○ **Handlebar Bag:** €19 weekly, with daily rates available.
- ○ **Panniers:** €29E weekly, with daily rates available.

Bike Rental in Munich Main Train Station

Overall Budget

All in, a day of riding (including hotel, bikes, food, local transportation) can be under €110 per day per person with two people sharing accommodations. This option is clearly far less than expensive organized bike tours that can be €800 or more per day per person. Trips can be made even easier by adding a local, organized day-ride tour, which might increase your trip cost by only €50 to €75 per person or less for a day's excursion.

The hotels I suggest throughout this book are generally not pricy, in many cases under €90 per night for a double, which always includes my fundamental requirement: a private bathroom and usually breakfast. Transportation by train or sightseeing boat is also a minimal additional cost, often under €15 for the rider and bike tickets required to return from a long day ride. Even with the occasional stay in a special hotel -- such as a chateau, a castle, or a hotel with a great pool or view -- the cost of these mini-adventures is far less than organized riding trips.

LOGISTICS: HOW TO GET AROUND

Given that none of these rides are designed to be supported by a tour guide or vehicle, the logistic support is provided by trains, and to a lesser degree, sightseeing river boats. Here are a few tips on how to best use these forms of logistical support:

Why Use This Support:

- **To Start and Finish a Ride**: We often use trains to get to our starting point on the ride, or from the end point of the ride back to our hotel after a one-way ride. Some rides suggested in this book include train rides to the beginning and from the end of the ride, as in the ride through the Wachau Valley along the Danube River when staying in Vienna.
- **Equalize Riders**: Trains and boats can be used to help equalize riders, allowing some riders to go further while others to meet them at a designated location.
- **Additional Base Locations**: Trains are handy to move to another base hotel location for extended combination day-riding vacations.
- **Shorten Rides**: Trains and boats can facilitate shorter rides -- you don't have to do the full routes outlined in each chapter to enjoy these day rides!

Bike Trains and Reservations:

- Not all trains allow bikes onboard, and some don't allow tandems.
- This limitation is especially true for high-speed trains. Even some local trains require reservations for bikes, which can be obtained at the ticket offices in train stations.
- If you know you will need a train segment for your trip, it is useful to reserve and purchase early (even before leaving home), which is often less costly and guarantees you a space on trains in which bike spaces can sell out.
- The cost of a ticket is for the passenger, and normally an additional ticket is required for the bike. Don't forget the bike

ticket so that you avoid potential fines and hassles.

- When boarding a train look for the train car with a bike painted on the side; these are designed for bikes and their riders. Most often they are in the rear of the train. Some stations have guides posted with a schematic for each train's configuration, and indicating where the bike cars will stop. Often you don't have much time to get aboard, since trains can stop for only a few minutes, so be prepared to race to the right spot quickly and load your bike.
- Download the terrific **DB Navigator app**, great for Germany, but also works in other parts of Europe. It provides train schedules, tracks, prices, all of which are very useful.

Buses:

Some countries have intercity buses with special bike trailers and racks, which are useful when no trains are available.

Sightseeing River Boats:

Sightseeing river tour boats can play a similar role to trains -- only more fun and scenic! These sightseeing boats operate on regular schedules, like trains, and are different than the large river cruise ships available for extended overnight trips (like Viking Cruises). Sightseeing river boats almost always allow bikes on board, and provide a great break during the day.

These boats also:

- Reduce mileage for a day.
- Provide a chance to see the scenery from the perspective of being on the river, which is especially attractive through river gorge areas.
- Allow you an opportunity to take a rest.
- Provide for time to have a meal or snack while cruising, with most boats having restaurants that serve surprisingly good food (be sure to try the apple strudel!).

Typical Tour Boat on Rhine

Ferries and River Crossings:

In many places, routes will take you across the river not by bridge but by other interesting methods, which might include large and small ferries or hydroelectric dams that also serve as pedestrian bridges. Being aware that these interesting opportunities might arise is important, so always:

- Keep in mind that sometimes, especially during offseason, smaller ferries might not be operating, so it is worth checking before your ride if you are depending on a certain crossing.
- Keep Euro coins ready for the short ferry rides, usually €1 to €2 per person including your bike.

NAVIGATION HINTS: GPS, NAVIGATION, AND MAPS

Navigating these rides is usually not difficult given that route signs are most often clearly posted, and you have the guidance of the river itself; big bodies of water easy to spot! That being said, having a digital map or app on your phone, as well as a large paper map for overall planning, are very useful. But even if more is not required, I like detailed maps and knowing as much as I can about a route. I always carry, at least, a good detailed roadmap covering the area.

Even better, consider obtaining specialized route maps, such as the *Bikeline* books (published by Esterbauer) that have terrific detailed directions and route information (with maps with detail down to every building on the route). The example below comes from the Wachau Valley along the Danube River. These books can often be purchased online from Amazon and other websites, including international European websites.

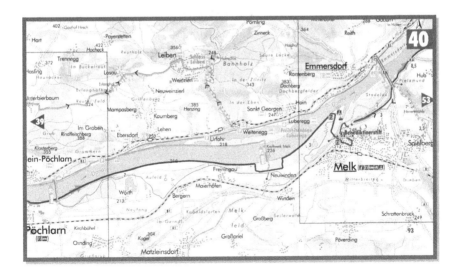

Extra navigation gear is useful -- I always take it -- but it is not necessary for these rides.

- **GPS and Navigation:** Consider bringing along a cycling GPS with digital map along, such as a Garmin 1030. The GPS will support navigation, of course, but also maintains ride statistics and history, and directs you to specific attractions and hotels.
- **Compass:** I always carry a compass. It is a good backup.
- **Phone Apps:** While I prefer a dedicated cycling GPS unit, there are many good options using a phone and a variety of apps. Here is a sample of these applications that can often be used offline as well as online:
  - Google Maps.
  - Komoot.
  - Ride With GPS.
  - Bikemap.

WHEN TO GO AND WEATHER CONSIDERATIONS

I admit I don't like riding in rain or cold, or into a strong headwind. If those conditions don't bother you, there is much more flexibility in deciding when and where to ride. But if they are relevant, please consider the following:

- **Seasons**: Spring tends to have more rain, so we like to ride in the late summer and throughout the fall.
- **Summer/Vacations**: Europeans vacation from July through mid-August, so hotels and sites are more crowded during this period. If you can avoid this period, there is less competition for hotels and rental bikes. But if you reserve hotels and bikes ahead, this period should not be a problem.
- **Wind**: Plan your trip so that you are riding with the prevailing wind behind you as much as possible. Use trains and boats to start routes upwind, if possible, for one-way routes. Check your weather app on your phone for wind direction for the few days you are planning your ride.
- **Local Weather Charts**: The best strategy is to study the average weather charts on places you are looking at riding to note average temperatures, rainfall, and wind directions.

SAFETY

Staying safe should always be the number one priority on a ride. Even on a short day ride, consider these recommendations on what to bring and use to stay safe.

- **Bright-Color Clothing**: Wear bright colors on the road. Bright yellow or green jerseys are highly recommended, if possible.
- **Good Helmets and Gloves**. These should be well-fitted, and consider the newer helmets with added safety features.
- **Lights**: Flashing lights are useful so consider bringing your own for your trip, even if riding during the daylight. These are small and easy to pack, and many have elastic strap on attachments for adding the lights to your rented bike.
- **Evacuation Insurance**: Not to scare you, but out of prudence it is never a bad idea to purchase an emergency medical evacuation policy. This is something you probably should have for your general trip (my friend broke a leg walking on some steps in Paris), but especially important for riding. Healthcare in Europe is usually quite good, often better than in the U.S., so this is not always necessary. On the other hand, if something does happen, you will likely want to get home as quickly as possible, and these policies can help. Not all policies are the same, read the fine print. I have found Medjet to provide reasonable flexibility.

THE RIDES

I have organized Part Two of this book along geographic regions, generally by country. The book focuses on rides along three main rivers (the Rhine, Danube, and Elbe), various routes that connect these rivers, a few smaller rivers that connect these rivers, and three lakes that provide especially enjoyable cycling. These connecting rivers include the Mosel, Neckar, Main, Inn, Loire, Adige, and Loire Rivers, and the lakes are Lake Bodensee, Lake Balaton, and Lake Neusiedl. Remember, too, that some rides also head away from rivers along country roads or bike trials, and in those cases, can involve more hill riding.

When selecting the location for your base hotel consider that some base locations offer three or more days of riding opportunities, while others have only one- or two-day rides suggested. No rides require an overnight stay away from your base hotel (though for two rides in this book I suggested a potential overnight). Only day bags are required, no larger bike panniers. Rides can often be shortened based on rider preferences.

As an option, day ride suggestions can be combined to give you the advantages of many days of diverse riding found in cycle touring, but without the need to carry everything you have on your bike or being part of an organized multi-day trip. Some base ride locations can also be combined to create a week or more of day rides, with only one or two hotel moves.

For example, you can easily combine (1) Trier and Koblenz, (2) Stuttgart and Strasbourg, or (3) Budapest, Bratislava, and Vienna.

As I mentioned earlier, the day rides recommended are far from the exhaustive list of rides available for each location -- there could be dozens of other good rides -- but the suggested rides tend to be along river, lake, and canal bike paths, making them safer, easier, and I would say, especially interesting.

The following symbols apply to each of the ride chapters in this book:

- ♥ Base Cities
- ⮠ Bike Rental
- 🏨 Hotels
- ⊤ Route Directions

GERMANY AND AUSTRIA

Germany has some of the best cycle paths in the world, and together with extensive rail and sightseeing boat infrastructure, it is one of my favorite cycling countries. Cycling Austria down the Danube River, the Inn River, and around Salzburg is also a fantastic experience.

The cities in this section are generally grouped by geographic proximity, but given that distances are often not that great, it is easy to get to almost any of these places from anywhere in Germany. You can also combine these rides into multi-day rides hosted from different base cities.

Here are the locations in Germany and Austria to stay and ride:

- ⚲ **Koblenz** – Located at the intersection of multiple rivers, Koblenz provides day rides on the Rhine, Mosel, and Lahn Rivers, including to the marvelous Castle Eltz and through the beautiful Rhine River Gorge.

- ⚲ **Rudesheim** – A charming town situated in the heart of the Rhine River Gorge and a UNESCO designated region.

- ⚲ **Trier** – The oldest city in Germany and site of extensive Roman ruins and attractions, located on the Mosel River and offering beautiful rides through lush vineyards.

- ⚲ **Heidelberg** – A fascinating city spared from the destruction of World War Two, providing splendid rides on the Neckar and Rhine Rivers.

- ⚲ **Frankfurt** – A financial center of Germany, offering great day rides on the Main River, including to the castle at Aschaffenburg, and short hops to the Rhine River.

- **Stuttgart** – This is the home of Mercedes and Porsche, and the associated fabulous automotive museums. It also provides special rides along the Neckar River to the historic university town of Tubingen and to the spa town of Bad Wimpfen.

- **Hamburg** – Stay in this dynamic city and ride the Elbe River toward the North Sea, or south through the former border between East and West Germany.

- **Bremerhaven** – Stay in this northern German city, enjoy the remarkable collection of special museums and rides to Bremen along the Weser River. Or head out along the North Sea to Cuxhaven and the end of the Elbe River.

- **Berlin/Potsdam** – Explore historic Potsdam and surrounding areas or ride all the way to Wittenberg on the Elbe River, which is where Martin Luther nailed his 95 Theses on the Castle Church helping to launch the Protestant Reformation.

- **Passau** – One of my favorites. A historic town with a fantastic university and ideally situated at the intersection of multiple rivers, including the Danube and Inn.

- **Munich** – The home of BMW and its museum -- with a short train journey to two scenic rides along the Inn River and historic walled towns.

- **Salzburg** – Rides along the quiet Salzach River that flows through Salzburg takes riders to the castle at Burghausen or to Bischofshofen. Alternatively, set out in a different direction to the beautiful cycling area around Chiemsee Lake.

- **Vienna** – Ride the Danube through the incredibly beautiful Wachau Valley – simply one of the best -- or go in the other direction to Bratislava and visit important Roman ruins along the way.

Koblenz Rides

Koblenz is an interesting city for a visit, and an exceptional cycling base that offers diverse and scenic rides on the Rhine, Mosel, and Lahn Rivers. Be sure to take the cable car across the Rhine to the Ehrenbreitstein Fortress, the second largest preserved fortress in Europe, and enjoy the views! It is easy to do four unique day rides from Koblenz, going in a different direction each day and staying at just one hotel. Longer and one-way rides work well from this base, as well, given the good train and boat infrastructure to support your return trips.

RIDE HIGHLIGHTS

+ Located in the heart of the Rhine Gorge, with its scenic historic towns and castles, providing up to four great days of day riding.

+ Take an excursion over the Rhine on the wonderful cable car ride to the Ehrenbreitstein Fortress.

+ Flexible routes with short and longer distances possible.

+ Multiple interesting destinations, including Bonn, Remagen (The Bridge Too Far), Rhine Gorge towns, Rudesheim, Eltz Castle, Cochem, and more.

+ **Getting There**: Located about an hour train ride from Frankfurt, Frankfurt Airport, Dusseldorf, Cologne, or Bonn.

Koblenz from Cable Car Over Rhine/Mosel Rivers   *Riding North of Koblenz along Rhine River Trail*

RIDE FEATURES

🏨 Hotels:

- I recommend staying along the Rhine River if budget and availability permit. There are many first-rate hotels to choose from, even in the smaller town of Lahnstein across the Rhine.
- Consider the Hotel Haus Morjan, which offers a good location on the Rhine River.
- The Mercure Hotel (also along the trail) is also well-placed and can be well-priced.

🚲 Bike Rental:

- Fahrradaus Zangmeister provides a good selection (www. Fahrrad-zangmeister.de).
- Micha's Rad-Atelier (info@rad-atelier.de).

RIDES

Given that multiple rivers intersect at Koblenz -- the Rhine, Mosel, and Lahn Rivers -- it can be a bit confusing when leaving Koblenz, so make sure you are on the right river. If you want to follow the Mosel, for example, be sure to cross at Schumacher Brucke.

┬ Koblenz to Bonn Rhine River North Ride

- Ride north along the west side of Rhine River bike trail to Bonn (65.5 km total). Train back to Koblenz.
- Koblenz to Bad Breisig (35 km). Breisig is a pleasant small town, and a good place for a stop to experience a smaller resort river town. Enjoy the restaurants along the embankment with good views of the river.
- Bad Breisig to Remagen (6.5 km). Consider a stop and explore this strategic location.

Seeing the Rhine River at Remagen reminds us of the strategic value of the Rhine River. The Rhine has long served as one of Europe's mighty natural barriers. There have been many famous crossings of the river, including dating back to the famous crossing of Julius Caesar in 55 BC using his amazing bridges.

Remagen is the location of a famous bridge over the Rhine River that proved one of the most important targets late in World War Two as the last bridge left standing across the river. The bridge was captured by the Allies, and was later a subject of a movie, *The Bridge at Remagen*. Be sure to visit the small museum.

- Remagen to Bonn (24 km). Explore this former capital of West Germany, a great potential dinner or lunch location before heading back to Koblenz by a train ride that takes less than one hour.

✝ Koblenz to Rudesheim Rhine River South Ride

- Riding south on the Rhine River from Koblenz, through a UNESCO designated area, this route offers many beautiful views and idyllic small river towns.
- The bike trail is often good on both sides of the Rhine River, permitting round-trip rides, or even two days of day rides, with each day spent on a different side of the river.
- Numerous stops for lunch, coffee, pastries, beer, and more.
- I also suggest riding south toward Rudesheim (64 km total).
- The overall distance can be adjusted using trains, or even better, by taking a cruise on one of the many sightseeing river boats.
- Towns of special mention along this route include Oberwesel, Boppard, Bingen, Rudesheim, Kaub, St. Gore, and Bacharach.
- Rudesheim is one of my favorite Rhine River towns, with attractive old streets, wine gardens, and interesting music and wine museums. Check out the Siegfried's Mechanical Museum, showcasing over 300 self-playing mechanical musical instruments.
- Train back to Koblenz in less than an hour.

Bike Trail along the Rhine River near Boppard   *Cochem Along the Mosel*

✝ Koblenz to Cochem Mosel River Ride

- The Mosel River provides for beautiful riding all the way to Metz in France and through the historic town of Trier, which is discussed later in this book.
- Consider a ride from Koblenz to Cochem, a medieval city about 48 km from Koblenz. I like the stretch of the Mosel River between Cochem and Trier, but this first leg of the ride is well-worth the pedaling.
- Head out along the Mosel River along the northwest side of the river, toward Winningen, and then Kobern-Gondorf, to Moselkern. Consider a stop at the world-class Eltz Castle along the way, though getting up to the Castle involves considerable hill climbing. Consider leaving your bike in the town of Moselkern, along the river, and take taxi to castle (about €30 roundtrip).

Eltz Castle

The Eltz Castle is one of the few medieval castles never destroyed or rebuilt, and owned by same family since 1157.

We rode to Moselkern, and since we were with my 86 year old uncle, we took the cab up and spent a couple hours exploring the castle and surrounds. It would have been a tough ride up!

- Continue past Treis-Karden to Cochem.
- Enjoy the medieval town of Cochem and visit the Reichsburg Cochem Castle, the Bundesbank-Bunker fall-out shelter, and museums.
- Train or boat back to Koblenz, just over an hour ride.

Perched above the historic city of Cochem, the Reichsburg Cochem was first built in the 12th century, and served as a toll gate for those passing through on the Mosel River below.

The castle was later destroyed, but rebuilt during the period of 1868-1877. If you have time, consider a guided tour that will take you back to Cochem's Medieval heritage.

✝ Koblenz to Limburg Lahn River Ride

- Ride from Koblenz to Limburg (about 59 km) on the Lahn River, starting across the Rhine River from Koblenz. This ride involves some hills, detours off the river at points, and sometimes involves unpaved pathways, so in some ways this is the most challenging day ride presented from Koblenz. But it is well worth the expedition.
- Start at Lahnstein, near the intersection of the Rhine and Lahn rivers across from Koblenz, and head East on the Lahn River.
- Arrive at Bad Ems, a spa city, after about 13 km. This is also the location of the "Ems Dispatch," which played a role in the beginning of the Franco-Prussian War of 1870.
- Continue pedaling past several attractive small towns, Nassau, Obernhof, Laurenburg, and arrive at Limburg. Take a few hours to explore Limburg, a medieval town, with half-timbered houses, and 12th century cathedral.
- A few kilometers past Limburg find the pleasant town of Diez with historic castle.
- Train back to Koblenz, just over an hour journey.

Rudesheim Rides

Rudesheim is a charming base town providing up to four days of excellent day riding. Like the rides from Koblenz, the cycling from Rudesheim provides interesting history and sites, beautiful scenery, short or longer distances, and easy logistics. Rudesheim is one of my favorite Rhine River towns, with great old streets, wine gardens, and interesting music and wine museums. Check out the Siegfried's Mechanical Museum.

RIDE HIGHLIGHTS

✦ Located in the heart of the Rhine Gorge, with its scenic towns and castles; a UNESCO World Heritage Site.

✦ Great train and boat infrastructure.

✦ Bike-friendly hop on-and-off sightseeing river boats.

✦ Flexible routes with short and longer distances possible.

✦ **Getting There**: Less than an hour train ride Frankfurt or the Frankfurt Airport.

Rudesheim on the Rhine River

Bike Trail Along the Rhine River near the Lorelei

RIDE FEATURES

🏨 Hotels:

- Consider the Hotel Linderwirt, which is friendly, historic, has a wine garden, and is located in a lively area in the center of town.

🚲 Bike Rental:

- Radkranz (www.rad-kranz.com). The also provide luggage transfer and other services.

RIDES

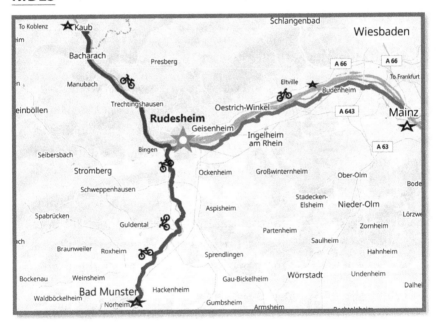

✝ Rhine-Mainz Ride

- Round-trip ride, starting on one side of Rhine River and heading to Mainz, and then back on the other side of the Rhine River through Bingen (72 km total), or consider a one-way ride to Mainz and train or boat back (36 km).
- Ride along the Rhine east toward Mainz.
- Stop in Eltville, a center of the wine trade and an attractive castle, at about the 16 km mark.

33

- Proceed along the Rhine River to the outskirts of Wiesbaden (Bierbrich), past stately homes, to the Schloss Bierbrich on the Rhine, which is a castle built in 1702.
- Continue along the Rhine River, then cross the river to Mainz. Explore the city if you have time (especially the Romanesque cathedral of St. Stephen and the Gutenberg Museum), then proceed back toward Rudesheim on the southwest side of the Rhine River. Alternatively, you can take the train back.
- On the ride back continue past Ingelheim, site of a former castle of Charlemagne, and through the Rheinauen nature reserve.
- At Bingen take ferry across the Rhine River back to Rudesheim.

Siegfried's Mechanical Museum

My son was nine when we first went to the wonderful Siegfried Mechanical Museum in Rudesheim. He played the violin and was enchanted by the many exhibits and working music machines.

We all enjoyed seeing 350 self-playing mechanical music instruments built over the last 300 years. Violins, pianos, and more playing without a human musician.

To me, the most fun was seeing how these clever mechanical contraptions worked -- in some ways they are like early computers using a form of data storage to play various instruments. A terrific stop in Rudesheim for young and old alike!

☨ World Heritage Rhine River Ride

- This is a beautiful ride northwest along the Rhine River and full of castles, charming towns, and river cruises. It is **simply one of the best cycle routes anywhere!**

- There are 57 km to 80 km round-trip options as well as many other combinations for shorter or longer rides along this route.
- Consider shorter rides and make the ride round-trip, a one-way with a great river cruise return, or a long ride all the way to Koblenz (64 km) and train or boat back.
- Given that the bike trail is generally terrific on both sides of the river, riding one day on each side of the river is also an option, with a train or boat return trip always an option.
- Consider stops in Bingen, Lorch, Bacharach (16 km), Kaub, Oberwesel (22 km), passing the legendary Loreley passage (steep slate rocks, home of stories of a beautiful siren enchanting passing sailors with song), to St. Gore (29 km from Rudesheim), and Boppard (additional 11 km). Each of these is a great location for a food and beverage stop as well as some wandering around historic small towns.
- I recommend riding at least as far as St. Gore, and seeing its Burge Rheinfels Castle, the largest ruin on the Middle Rhine River. This route also provides an opportunity for a ride through the Loreley.
- Long walks without a bike are another pleasant option along this route, especially for non-riding companions.

Kaub on the Rhine River Gorge   *Near Boppard*

✝ Nahe River Ride

- This is a relatively easy ride along the smaller Nahe River, which flows into the Rhine River opposite Rudesheim. It is 29 km one-way with train return to Bingen, or 57 km round-trip.
- Take the passenger ferry across the Rhine near Quay 8.
- Cycle past Bingen, past Bad Kreuznach with its bridge houses, to the town of Bad Munster am Stein-Ebernburg.
- Bad Munster is a smaller town with resort hotels and mineral spring spas (try the Rheingrafenstein thermal outdoor pool after your ride!).
- Enjoy the Rotenfels rock formation and views of the river valley, and take in the sight of the Rheingrafenstein if you would like a short climb.

Trier Rides

Trier is a fascinating city -- Germany's oldest -- with rich history, including one of the best locations in this book to visit and explore Roman ruins. Located along the Mosel River, near the Luxembourg border, Trier served as the center of the Western Roman Empire, with a population that might have reached 100,000 by the 4th century (Augusta Treverorum). Explore a first-rate collection of Roman ruins, including one of the city's main gates, the Porta Nigra, the Roman baths, an amphitheater, and an archeological museum. Trier is a great city for riding, but also for keeping non-riders busy.

RIDE HIGHLIGHTS

+ Roman ruins (headquarters for Rome in this region) and museums in ancient city of Trier.

+ Great Rides along the Mosel River and other rides.

+ Ride through beautiful vinyards and sample many German white wines -- Riesling Grand tour.

+ Visit an amazing World War Two Maginot Line installation and museum.

+ Consider pairing this ride with Koblenz-based rides, which provides seven or eight days of good riding with only two hotels!

+ **Getting There**: Train from Frankfurt (2.5 hours) or closer to Koblenz or Luxembourg City.

Roman Porta Nigra in Trier *Along the Mosel River Route*

RIDE FEATURES

🏨 Hotels:

- The Mercure Hotel is directly across from the Porta Nigra, with many rooms having wonderful views of this spectacular ancient Roman gate.
- Consider the Hotel Villa Hugel, built in 1914, for its 36 rooms, good views, pool, and great breakfast. It is only a 10 minute walk from the city center.

🚲 Bike Rental:

- Fahrradstation, located in the Trier train station, with a good variety, including 8-speed, 27-speed, and e-bikes (www. fahrradstation.bues-trier.de).

RIDES

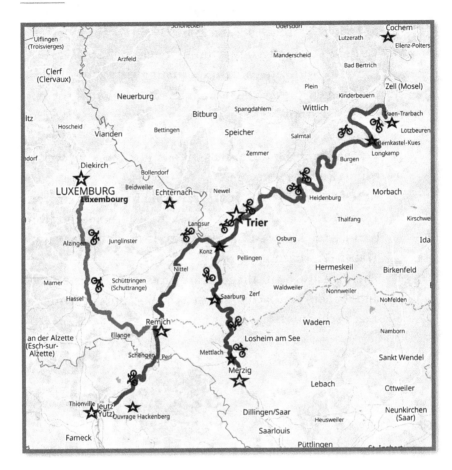

I recommend the Bikeline *Velo Route Saarlor Lux* map book for this area if you are going to pursue rides that take you off the well-marked, relatively easy, Mosel River route. The *Bikeline Mosel River* book is also useful.

✝ Grand Mosel Ride

- Head northeast on the Mosel River to the attractive city of Bernkastel-Kues (59 km). There is an option to continue further to Traben-Trarbach (total 80 km).
- Follow route signs. If using the *Bikeline* route, initially stay on the south side of Mosel River; it can be a bit confusing

until Ruwer, then to Bernkastel-Kues stay on the Map "E" side of the Mosel (if using *Bikeline* maps). Bernkastel-Kues to Traben-Trarbach stay on Map "G" side of the Mosel.

- This route is through my favorite stretch on the Mosel River, complete with vineyards and stunning views.
- Bernkastel-Kues is the more interesting town of the two potential stops, with a visit to the wine museum worth the time.
- Traben-Trarbach has cycle and toy museums -- as well as a huge Buddha Museum.
- Note: it is an easy 1.2-hour train ride back to Trier from Traben-Trarbach, but bus connections are needed from Bernkastel-Kues, so I recommend riding all the way to Traben-Trarbach.
- There are also boats that operate between Bernkastel-Kues and Traben-Trarbach to shorten the ride, but remember to check schedules.

Bike Trail Along the Mosel River   *Leaving Trier along the Mosel River*

⼦ Mosel Toward Thionville Ride:

- Ride along the Mosel River toward Luxembourg (south) to Remich (40 km), continue further to Perl (Germany), or Schengen in Luxembourg (50 km).
- Consider riding further to the French town of Thionville (78 km).
- Both rides take you through the attractive town of Remich, which is worth a stop.

- Take the train ride back (One hour plus).
- If you ride all the way to Thionville, there is a special reward of visiting the Ouvrage Hackenberg Maginot line installation. Note there is climbing involved to get there, as you ride away from the river. The best route is from Koenigsmacker on the trail near road D2 and head toward Budling on the D61. I would suggest an early start from Trier if you want to have time for this stop, and confirm tour times before leaving Trier.

The Ouvrage Hackenberg Maginot Line fortification is the largest dating from before World War Two. The Maginot Line was built by the French in the 1930s in an effort to protect them from a future German invasion. In many ways, it was built upon the lessons of World War One and its trench warfare, and proved totally unsuited to the swift mechanical attack of the Germans in the Second World War.

This line of fortifications was quickly bypassed and isolated by the Germans, and most ended up surrendering. The bullet holes you will see on this fortification were fired by American guns as they fought to retake these fortifications from the Germans who assumed these positions after the French rapid surrender.

Take the fascinating two-hour English tour during some afternoons, including rides on the original underground rail system.

✝ Saar River Ride.

- This interesting route takes you along the Mosel River to the Saar River.
- Head southwest along the Mosel River from Trier to Konz, and then as the river divides, take the Saar River south.
- Ride along the Saar River to Saarburg (21 km).
- Continue to Mettlach (additional 19 km, total 40 km), with a few hills when entering the city, which is headquarters for Villeroy & Boch. Plan a 35-minute train ride back to Trier.
- Consider an additional 17.5 km to Merzig, where you can visit the local museum and castle. Schedule for about a one-hour train back to Trier.

We took a guided walking tour around Trier operated by the local tourist office, highly recommended. One of the fun facts we learned was that Trier is the birthplace of Karl Marx. Not sure how this anti-capitalist would feel about his ancestral home now ironically serving as a Dollar Store!

✝ Trier to Luxembourg City Ride

- There are multiple routes between Trier and Luxembourg city, but I recommend the 77-km route provided herein. Some options are more direct and shorter but involve more road riding. Riding to Luxembourg City is generally a more challenging ride than most in this book, but a worthwhile adventure.
- Ride southwest on the Mosel toward Luxembourg and France (away from Koblenz).
- Trier to Langsur (15 km) leaving the Mosel River at Wasserbillig to the Sauer River.
- Langsur to Echternach (19 km).
- Echternach to Beidweiler (30.5 km), with some hills

Echternach makes a good meal stop.

- Beidweiler to Luxembourg (25 km) with some hills.
- Alternatively, ride to Remich (40 km), then 30 km further to Luxembourg City, from Remich through Ellange, Hassel, and Alzingen, on a somewhat hilly route.
- Explore this larger capital city with historic and newer city sections, many restaurants and museums, and then take a short train ride back to Trier.

Heidelberg Rides

Heidelberg is one of the special towns in Europe, located along the Neckar River. It was not destroyed during World War Two, meaning it has retained its historic, albeit touristy, charm. Heidelberg is an easy train ride from Frankfurt and other parts of Western Europe, and is a terrific place to spend some time and do a bit of riding. There are many attractions, including the must-see Heidelberg Castle (hike up and enjoy the views), the Old Bridge (Karl Theordor Bridge dating from 1788), the Church of the Holy Spirit, and the Heidelberg University. I recommend a pair of day rides in this town, but you could certainly enjoy more.

RIDE HIGHLIGHTS

+ Beautiful city of Heidelberg.

+ Plenty to do and see in this historic town.

+ Beautiful Neckar River valley ride.

+ Good train and boat infrastructure.

+ **Getting There**: Train from Frankfurt (1.5 to 2 hours depending on the train), about the same from the Frankfurt Airport. A bit more than an hour train ride from Stuttgart.

Heidelberg

Ride along the Neckar River

RIDE FEATURES

⊞ Hotels and More:

- The Hotel Hollander Hof, central location with Neckar River views, has a pleasant staff and good breakfast at a reasonable price for relatively expensive city (www.hollaender-hof.de).
- Try the Cordon Bleu at the Restaurant Goldener Hecht, next door, or one of 100 different schnitzels at the Schnitzelhaus Alte Munz.

🚲 Bike Rental:

- Joyrides, e-bike specialists (www.joyrides-rent.de).
- Heidel Bike, bike shop and rentals (www.heidel-bike.de).

RIDES

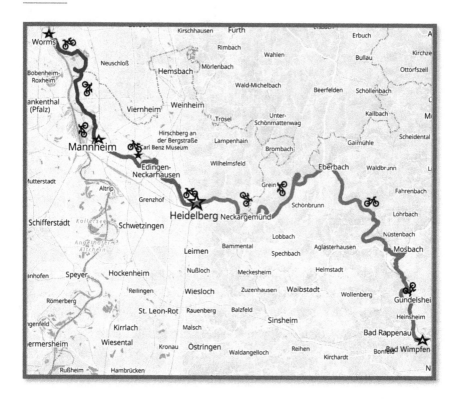

✝ Heidelberg to Bad Wimpfen Ride

- This is a beautiful ride to Bad Wimpfen, with numerous vineyards and castles found along the Neckar River (total ride 80 km). There are also shorter distance options along the way with train and round-trip riding options. The train back from Bad Wimpfen is between about one hours plus depending on the train you catch.

- Also consider joining a Neckar River sightseeing boat for part of your journey, either departing in the morning from Heidelberg or climbing aboard the boat later in the ride. Always remember to check the schedules.

- Heidelberg to Hirschhorn (25 km). Follow the directions carefully on the way to Kleingemund, and consider a stop for a great pastry, coffee, or beer stop.

- At Hirschhorn consider a climb to the Schlosshotel Liebenstein, and a coffee and strudel on its beautiful roof terrace -- you will deserve it after the climb up!
- Hirschhorn to Neckargerach (21 km).
- Neckargerach to Bad Wimpfen (30.5 km).
- Explore the charming medieval old town of Bad Wimpfen, with half-timbered houses, and visit the Staufen Imperial Palace and the Blauer Turm (Blue Tower) from the 13th century. Be sure to climb to the top if it is open to the public.
- Highly recommended: a dip into the public hot spring spa adjacent to the Rosengarten Hotel -- a great way to end a ride!

Hirschhorn on the Neckar River

View from Bad Wimpfen

The Heidelberg Castle was begun in the 13th century. Lightning destroyed the upper castle in 1537, and it was further damaged by fire and war. A cycle of destruction and rebuilding has left an interesting combination of architecture reflecting centuries of renovations.

One of my favorite spots is the Heidelberg Tun in the Castle, the incredibly large wine vat dating from the 18th century – they had their priorities straight!

✝ Heidelberg to the Rhine Ride

- Heidelberg to Mannheim on the Neckar River to the Rhine River (24 km each way) makes an enjoyable one-way ride with train back, or great round-trip ride.

- The route from Heidelberg is straightforward, first on the northwest side of the Neckar River, and then at Ladenburg, crossing the river to the other side. At Ladenburg, consider a stop at the Carl Benz museum for a look at the early automobiles (his home before moving to Stuttgart).

- If you want to go further, turn north on the Rhine River and ride to Worms (another 24 km), staying on the east side of the Rhine River until crossing at Worms.

- If continuing to Worms, at Mannheim first ride through the old city, then cross the Kurpfalz Bridge. The confluence of the Rhine and Neckar Rivers can be a bit confusing with multiple bridges in this industrial area, so pay special attention.

- Ride north along the Rhine River staying near the river (note there is a bridge or ferry that can be used to cross the small river north of the city), then follow the route to Lampertheim, and then head back generally toward to river, crossing the Rhine at a bridge into Worms at Rosengarten.

- Worms is one of the oldest cities in Germany, and known for the Diet of Worms of 1521, when authorities met to debate how to respond to Martin Luther. An hour train trip takes you back to Heidelberg.

Frankfurt Rides

Whether you fly into Frankfurt to start your European holiday, are touring this interesting town on vacation, or are there on business, Frankfurt offers the opportunity to enjoy some wonderful day rides on the Main River, and even the Rhine River. The Main River flows through the city and offers rides through small towns and provides easy logistics. Lesser known than the Rhine or Mosel Rivers, the Main River offers special cycling routes in its own right.

RIDE HIGHLIGHTS

✦ Two exciting day rides presented exploring the Main River, one taking you to the Rhine River.

✦ Mixture of small and larger towns.

✦ Aschaffenburg and its palace.

✦ Easy place to add some riding when flying into Europe at Frankfurt Airport.

Along the Main River in Frankfurt

Castle in Aschaffenburg

RIDE FEATURES

⊞ Hotels:

- There are so many hotels in Frankfurt to choose from, so your choice depends on budget and purpose of your trip.
- The AMERON Frankfurt Neckarvillen Boutique hotel is one with some character and good location.
- At the Airport there are several hotels, including the better-priced Hilton Garden Inn or Sheraton Hotel.

🚲 Bike Rental:

- There are many bike rental shops in Frankfurt, so here are a couple of suggestions.
- Frankfurt Bike Tour (www.frankfurtbiketour.com) offers a variety of bikes, including e-bikes, children's bikes, and child bike carriers.
- Electric Bike Frankfurt, specializing in a variety of different types of e-bikes for rent (www.electric-bike-frankfurth.com).

RIDES

𐤕 Mainz Ride

- Frankfurt to Mainz along the Main river, and merging with the Rhine River near Mainz, is an attractive route (35 km each way).
- Consider riding one-way, with an easy train back to Frankfurt, or a round-trip ride.
- Hochheim makes a good stop, famous for its Riesling wine.
- Once you are at the Rhine across from Mainz, consider an additional 14.5 km west on the Rhine River to the attractive small town of Eltville am Rhein for a stroll and snack, and train back or make it a longer round-trip ride.

𐤕 Main River Ride

- Ride along the Main River from Frankfurt to Aschaffenburg (53 km), with the option to train back or make a long round-trip.
- Head out of Frankfurt along the Main River bike trail west, and then southwest, away from the Rhine River.

- Downtown Frankfurt to Offenbach (6.5 km). Offenbach is worth a visit, including Isenburger Schloss. You will be riding on the south side of the Main River during this portion of the trip.
- Offenbach am Main to Seligenstadt (30 km). Both Steinheim and Kesselstadt are worth a stop and can be great destinations for a day ride (with a train ride back), or a turnaround point for a round-trip ride back to Frankfurt. From Hainstadt to Aschaffenburg there is a bike trail on both sides of the Main River.
- Seligenstadt to Aschaffenburg (18 km). From Mainflingen, cross the bridge to the east side of the Main River toward Dettingen, then proceed toward Mainaschaff and onward to Aschaffenburg.
- In Aschaffenburg and visit the palace.
- Quick train back to Frankfurt.

The imposing Johannisburg Palace and Gardens in Aschaffenburg was originally built 1605-1614, as the second residence of the Prince Bishop of Mainz. The red sandstone exterior gives the palace its color. The palace was nearly destroyed by U.S. forces near the close of World War Two, and took 20 years to rebuild to its current condition. Try the cafe restaurant in front of palace facing the river.

✝ Rhine Ride Option

- It is easy to also take day rides along the Rhine River from Frankfurt, with short train rides to the beginning and from the end of the rides available. Consider a train to Rudesheim and enjoy some of the rides suggested in the Rudesheim chapter.

Stuttgart Rides

Whether you are visiting or passing through Stuttgart -- or perhaps picking up a new car for European delivery -- Stuttgart provides two excellent day rides along the Neckar River. Make sure to visit the amazing Mercedes Museum, and also enjoy the smaller Porsche Museum. The 363-km Neckar River provides for some excellent riding, including the rides presented in the Heidelberg section of this book. In this chapter, find rides either to the historic university town of Tubingen or to the attractive spa town of Bad Wimpfen.

RIDE HIGHLIGHTS

+ Beautiful rides through vinyards along the Neckar River.

+ Bad Wimpfen, and enjoy a soak in a local spa.

+ Tubingen, a smaller medieval town, with historic university. Great for walking and exploring.

+ **Getting There:** Fly in or train from Frankfurt (2.3 hours) or Munich (2.2 hours).

Original Model at Porsche Museum   *Porsche Museum*

RIDE FEATURES

⊞ Hotels and More:

- Consider staying at the Hilton Garden Inn, which is walking distance from the fabulous Mercedes-Benz Museum and right off the bike trail, though there are numerous hotels in Stuttgart, many closer to the town center than this location.
- If staying at the Hilton Garden Inn, enjoy dinner at the nearby pig museum and restaurant -- yes that's right -- a short walk across the Rhine River. Look for the Schweinemuseum and enjoy a memorable meal in a fascinating venue.

The last time we enjoyed the Schweinemuseum's wonderful restaurant a well-intended waitress balancing two liters of beer in each hand tripped causing a minor waterfall to pour down my unfortunate son's back. The staff was horrified, and did their best. My son remained a trooper, helped along by a free, dry, pig museum shirt (he is the only kid in his school with one of those!) and unlimited chocolate cake. A memorable meal!

🚲 Bike Rental:

- Stuttgart By Bike offers large variety of bikes and e-bikes (www.stuttgart-by-bike.com).

RIDES

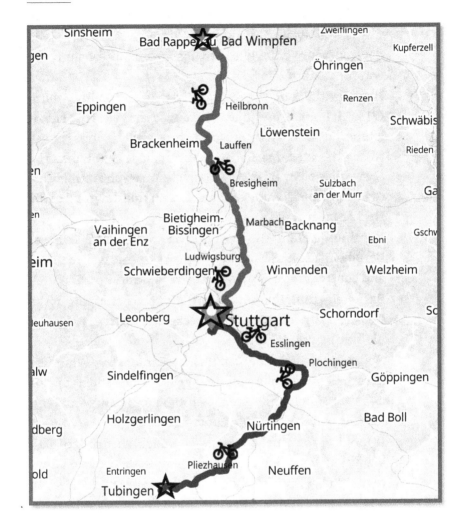

🕂 Bad Wimpfen Neckar River Ride.

- This ride is quite scenic, with vinyards, castles, and attractive towns. Make it all the way to Bad Wimpfen (83 km for a long day), or stop at cities like Ludwigsburg, or others along the way for a shorter day.

- Head north along the Neckar River toward Ludwigsburg (21 km). If you want to leave the river and visit the city, it is uphill, but is an interesting stop with an opportunity to see the amazing Ludwigsburg Palace, known as the "Versailles of Swabia." Alternatively, take a short train ride to Ludwigsburg, enjoy the Palace, then ride downhill to the Neckar River trail.

- Continuing along the Neckar River from Ludwigsburg to Besigheim (26 km). Stop in Besigheim (scenic walled town) and consider returning to Stuttgart (45-minute train ride).

- Besigheim to Heilbronn (24 km). Consider stopping at the Deutsches Zweirad Museum in Neckarsulm and its fascinating historic bicycle exhibit.

- Heilbronn to Bad Wimpfen (13 km). Explore Bad Wimpfen. Recommended: Take a plunge at the springs and hot pools near the Hotel am Rosengarten (Solebad Bad Wimpfen), making it convenient for a post-ride soak.

- If looking for a post-ride meal, snack, or drink in Bad Wimpfen, consider the Lukulos Am Blauen Turm Greek restaurant with reasonable food, good beer and deserts, and a beautiful view from its terrace overlooking the river.

- Relax on the train ride back to Stuttgart (about 1.2 hours).

Riding along the Neckar Trail   *Tubingen English Tour*

The Mercedes-Benz Museum is a must see in Stuttgart. Opened in 2006, and located within a fabulous piece of architecture, the museum contains over 160 vehicles of all types.

View everything from the first cars ever built to the Popemobile. One of the most interesting features of the museum is how the history of the company and automobiles is connected with a general historical timeline to keep everything in context, including the darker period in the company's history during World War Two.

✝ Tubingen Neckar River Ride

- Embark on this 63-km ride, exiting Stuttgart heading southwest along the Neckar River trail, through an industrial part of town, with the ride becoming increasingly scenic after several kilometers.
- Stuttgart to Nurtingen (34 km).
- Nurtingen to Tubingen (29 km). Stop for lunch or snack at Seehaus Neckarhausen, which is right on the trail. Tubingen is an attractive town worth an extended visit.

- I recommend the walking tour (in English) on Saturday mornings from the tourist center.
- TransVelo bike shop for repairs, near the Ibis Hotel.
- Less than an hour train ride back to Stuttgart.

Tubingen is known for its university founded in 1477, and especially renowned for theology and medical studies. With over 20,000 students, it is located within a beautiful medieval city, which like Heidelberg, was largely undamaged in World War Two.

Check out the pigeon population-control bird house near the river, where pigeons are lured to enter with the prospect of food and housing, only to have their eggs removed to maintain a check on pigeon populations.

I feel it is necessary to mention that the town also had a dark period during Nazi Germany, when it was a center for racial studies and gruesome medical experiments.

Hamburg Rides

Hamburg is a fascinating and dynamic city to visit and well-worth exploring by bike, especially the redeveloped waterfront and the central park. Hamburg is one of my favorite major German cities -- so long as not too deep into the colder Fall. If you have additional time in the city, consider these two great day rides along the Elbe River.

RIDE HIGHLIGHTS

+ Head south along the Elbe River, following the former border area between East and West Germany.

+ Head north along the Elbe River to where the Elbe meets the North Sea, stopping at the historic town of Stade, and then finishing at the resort beach area of Cuxhaven option.

Hamburg Riverfront

Elbe flowing into the North Sea

RIDE FEATURES

🏨 Hotels:

- There are many hotels throughout Hamburg, but consider the three-star Hotel Stella Maris, near the waterfront, which is a great location.

🚲 Bike Rental:

- Zweiradperle. A large variety of bikes available (www.zweiradperle.hamburg/bike-rental).
- ERFAHRE Hamburg, e-bike specialists (www.efahre.com).

RIDES

✝ Hamburg along the Elbe River to Stade Route

- There are cycling routes on both sides of the Elbe River as you head northwest out of Hamburg, but I suggest crossing the river near Hamburg at Othmarschen by ferry, and heading to the town of Stade on the southern side of the Elbe (45 km one way).
- Continue along the river route heading away from the river at Bassenfleth and toward Stade.
- Enjoy exploring the wonderful town of Stade for a couple of hours, then a one-hour train ride back to Hamburg.

Stade   *Bike Trail Near Cuxhaven*

✝ Stade to Cuxhaven Route

- It is a long ride from Hamburg to Cuxhaven on the North Sea Coast, but with an extra train ride it is more accessible. I suggest taking the one-hour train to Stade, explore this terrific city, then head out of town on your bike generally along the Elbe River to Cuxhaven.
- This ride is 76 km, and if you have extra energy, continue past Cuxhaven, and explore the end of the Elbe River as it empties into the North Sea, and take a brisk dip at the nearby beaches.
- This ride does involve double train trips given the start in Stade and finish in Cuxhaven, but this allows riders to explore the terrific city of Stade, and the beautiful end of the Elbe River as it flows into the North Sea, with beaches

that come and go with the extreme local tides. Consider a horse-and-cart ride far out to sea during low tide!

- Train back to Hamburg (1.75 hours).

 We really could not believe our eyes—horses and carriages parading hundreds of meters off the beach on the flats left from a receding tide.

These trips are easy to book, and can cover up to 12 km taking as little as an hour travelling between the Weser and Elbe Rivers. In cooler weather blankets are provided. We didn't have time for an excursion, but definitely next time!

✝ Hamburg along the Elbe River to Lauenburg Route

- Take this 44-km ride one-way with a train back or a longer round-trip ride.
- Head south along the Elbe River then follow the route to Oschsenwerder and then Geesthacht (26 km), often a few hundred meters away from the Elbe River. Explore Geesthacht and perhaps have a snack.
- Continue along the river to Lauenburg, with small parts of this section not paved (18 km).
- Visit interesting city of Lauenburg followed by a 1.2-hour train ride back to Hamburg.

Bremerhavan Rides

Bremerhaven is a port city, like Hamburg, and served as the departure port for many European immigrants sailing to North America. Because of its strategic nature, Bremerhaven was largely destroyed during World War Two by bombing. The city rebuilt and added one special feature -- a collection of interesting museums. The Immigration Museum (Deutsches Auswandererhaus), the first-class Climate Museum, and the Maritime museum are all recommended. I am suggesting two attractive rides from Bremerhaven: one along the North Sea coast to Cuxhaven, and the other south along the Weser River to Bremen.

RIDE HIGHLIGHTS

+ Great museums to enjoy when not riding and for non-riders.

+ North Sea seafood and port environment smaller than Hamburg.

+ Visit the interesting city of Bremen.

+ Explore the North Sea coast, beaches, small towns, and striking scenery.

+ Cycle along the smaller Weser River.

+ **Getting There:** Train from Hamburg (under 2 hours) or from Bremen (35 minutes).

Bremerhaven Maritime Museum

Hotel Atlantic in Bremerhaven

RIDE FEATURES

Hotels:

- For a stay with a view, in the center of the port, and near museums, consider the Atlantis Hotel (www.atlantic-hotels. de). Other lower cost hotels also available.

Bike Rental:

- A good variety of bikes and e-bikes available from Fahrrad Vermietung in Wremen, which is about 5 km north of Bremerhaven (www.fahrradvertmietung-wremen.de).
- Some variety of bikes and e-bikes available at the Radstation (www.mietrad-bremerhaven.de).

RIDES

Consider the *Bikeline Weser-Radweg* book covering both these routes.

✝ North Sea Ride: Bremerhaven to Cuxhaven

- There are several towns to stop at along this route (54 km) to Cuxhaven.
- Head north from the city generally following a beautiful quiet bike trail mostly along the coast, with easy navigation.
- Enjoy small resort towns and stop at the beach.
- The large tide movements provided an opportunity for remarkable horse-and-cart rides far out to sea during low tide.
- Enjoy a 45-minute train ride back to Bremerhaven.

The climate museum (Klimahaus) in Bremerhaven was far ahead of its time, focusing on climate and climate change since opening in 2009, after more than a decade of planning. I have not seen anything else like it. Experience multiple climates and the climatic story. For example, in one area there is the heat and sand of the desert, and then around the corner the alpine climate of Switzerland, and so much more.

✝ Weser River Ride: Bremerhaven to Bremen.

- Attractive 75-km ride along the Weser River, heading south from this city.
- Consider taking a boat part of the way, check schedules (www.hal-oever.de).

Bike Trail North of Bremerhaven with Docks *Maritime Museum Bremerhavan*

- Cross the river to Blexen, and follow the Weser River trail generally south, with signs to Bremen.
- Near Bremen, past Woltmershausen, cross the bridge into Bremen.
- In Bremen, enjoy exploring the old town, and have a meal at the Ratswinkeller Restaurant, which has been serving food for over 600 years -- great atmosphere!
- Train back to Bremerhaven (35 minutes).

Berlin and Potsdam Rides

Berlin is one of the most fascinating and vibrant cities in Europe, once divided by its well-known wall, but also by a lesser-known undeveloped "buffer zone" between the city and what was the former West Germany. There are many day rides in Berlin, but I will focus on two through the historic areas around Potsdam and toward the Elbe River.

RIDE HIGHLIGHTS

✦ Ride to the interesting city of Potsdam and surrounding lakes and countryside.

✦ Travel through quiet areas that used to serve as a buffer between East and West, before German reunification, all the way to the Elbe River and Wittenberg, with its important role in the Reformation.

Berlin to Potsdam

Caputh near Potsdam

RIDE FEATURES

⛩ Hotels:

- There are many hotels in Berlin, so your choice depends on your interest and budgets.
- Alternative recommendation: Consider a country stay outside of Berlin, perhaps in Potsdam or in the attractive lakefront village of Caputh.
- In Caputh, consider the well-priced 3-star Mullerhof Hotel, though there are also many other more upscale hotels in this area and in Potsdam. Caputh is less than an hour train ride from Berlin, and is located next to a few lakes, making for a charming stay away from Berlin.

🚲 Bike Rental:

- Alex Rent-a-Bike, has a variety of bikes and also tours (Alex-rent-a-bike.de).
- There are also many bike sharing facilities in Berlin, but these services do not provide the higher-quality bike I usually recommend for longer rides.

RIDES

The following rides can depart from Berlin, from Potsdam or from Caputh, which is located about 10 km from Potsdam in the direction away from Berlin.

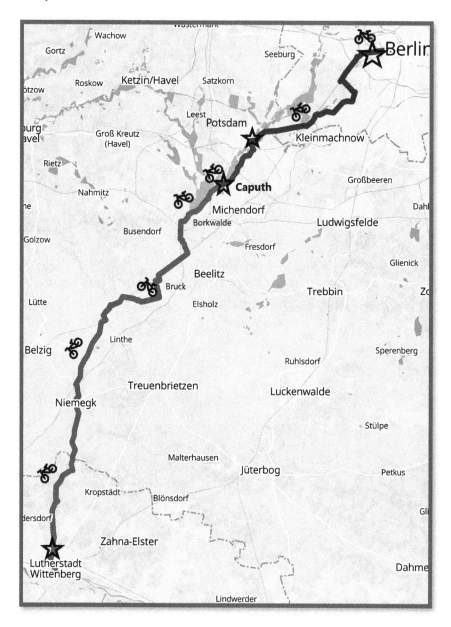

✝ Berlin to Potsdam.

- This 35-km ride to Potsdam takes riders out of Berlin, past the Brandenburg Gate, following Route 2, and then heading south at the Funkturm Berlin following Route 115 (Messedamm Road).
- After about 10 km of city riding, the route will pass through attractive park lands and lakes on its way to Potsdam.
- Potsdam is worth a few hours visit or more and is host to multiple sites, including the Sanssouci Palace dating back to Frederick the Great, as well as numerous gardens.

The Schloss Cecilienhof hosted the Potsdam Conference at the end of World War Two. At this conference Truman, Churchill and Stalin met during July to August 1945, to decide how to deal with Germany following its unconditional surrender in May. It was the first time the leaders met following the death of Roosevelt in April.

On your way from Berlin to Potsdam consider a stop at the Wannsee Villa, where in January 1942, Nazi leaders infamously met to plan the Final Solution and the extermination of the Jews in Europe.

Potsdam Fountain   *New Palace in Potsdam*

✝ Potsdam to Wittenberg.

- Depart from Potsdam or Caputh, or take train from Berlin to Potsdam in the morning and start your ride with a head start away from Berlin.
- There is bike trail along Route 2, but I prefer the 70-km route that takes riders through quite wooded pathways, often not paved, providing an insight into the former buffer zone between East and West. Be sure to take water and snacks with you since there are not many stops along this route.

 When riding from Caputh to the Elbe River, I knew I was close to Berlin, but I felt a million miles away with almost no buildings or people visible along the way. I am glad I brought plenty of snacks for this ride through the former East-West buffer zone.

- Head along the south side of the lakes, from Potsdam, past Caputh, to Schwielowsee toward Borkwalde, Bruck, Niemegk, and finally to Wittenberg on the Elbe River.
- Wittenberg is an historic town, especially famous with its connections to Martin Luther, including his house and the Stadtkirche, known as the Mother Church of the Reformation.
- Train back to Potsdam (1.5 hours) or Berlin (45 minutes). There are not great connections to Caputh, so train to Potsdam and ride 10 km back to Caputh.

Passau Rides

Known as the "Three River City of Passau," located at the confluence of the Danube, Inn, and Ilz rivers, Passau is one of my favorite cycling towns in Europe. It is a university center, with historic sites and many streets to explore, in both the old and new city areas. There is plenty to do for a four-day stay with multiple days of riding -- there is a reason Passau is one of the prime stops on the river-cruise ship circuit. Many sightseeing boat companies also operate on the Danube and Inn Rivers, providing opportunities for one-way rides and attractive cruises the other direction.

RIDE HIGHLIGHTS

+ Located at the border of Germany and Austria, provides great rides in both countries.

+ Fabulous rides on the Inn and Danube Rivers.

+ Great town to spend a couple of days when not cycling.

+ **Getting There**: Two-hour train ride from Munich. Also, near to Salzburg.

Passau along the Inn River   *Along Danube East of Passau*

RIDE FEATURES

▥ Hotels:

- I really like Hotel Wilder Mann in the center of town, which also houses a glass museum. Well-priced for the historical atmosphere and location. Simple accommodations, but rooftop breakfast room provides stellar views for starting the day (www.wilder-mann.com).
- The Hotel Faust Schloss in Aschach is a great stay if you decide for an overnight trip as described in this chapter.

ᯤ Bike Rental:

- There are many bike rental shops in Passau, so price them out and compare bike offerings. Here are two ideas:
- Fahrrad-Klinik Passau. Many choices, including e-bikes and tandems (www.fahrradklink-passau.de).
- Rent-A-Bike Passau offer many choices (www.bikeambulanz.de).
- Several companies offer bike tours from Passau, providing packages with multiple-day rides, and even luggage moving services if you would like to enjoy an easy point-to-point riding adventure for a few days from Passau.

RIDES

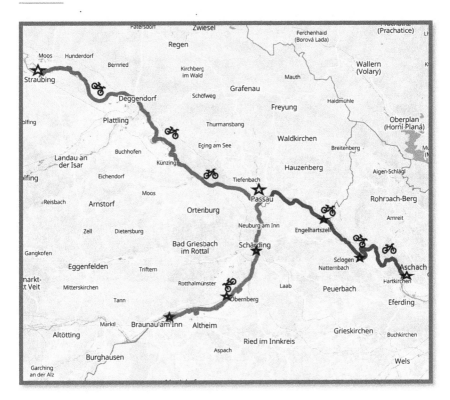

✝ Passau to Straubing Danube River Ride

- The ride to Straubing is 88.5-km ride, but there are also shorter options to Deggendorf or Vilshofen. Confirm train schedules before departing, with some fast trains available, but potentially with limited bike space.
- There are also sightseeing river boats operating on this stretch of the Danube, providing for one-way cycling, one-way cruise options, or shorter ride options. Check out the Donauschiffahrt sightseeing boat line company.
- Straubing is worth a couple hours for exploring, with its interesting history and especially its 14th-century gothic watchtower.
- A shorter roundtrip to Vilshofen ("The Small Three River City") is highly recommended (24 km each way), and with

the option of an additional route away from the river from Sandbach to Passau. The Benedictine Monastery Schweiklberg, consecrated in 1904, is located above the town.

Hotel Wilder-Mann   *Straubing Watchtower*

✝ Engelhartszell (Austria) Danube Ride:

- Enjoy a splendid day riding south along the Danube River to Engelhartszell.
- Pass the Castle Obernzell along the ride.
- Engelhartszell is a charming stop for lunch, and visit the Engelszell Abbey, which was founded in 1293.
- Ride the total 51.5-km round-trip, or take a sightseeing boat one-way from or to Passau to make it a shorter ride.

The Engelszell Abby is the only Trappist monastery in Austria, founded in 1293. The current building was built between 1754 and 1764.

✝ Passau-Austrian Danube Ride

- This is a favorite ride I have enjoyed many times, 67 km to Aschach, and then beyond. The problem is there are not great train connections back to Passau from Aschach. Here are some options:
  - Ride an additional 24 km -- I know, 91 km is a lot of riding. Arrive at Linz for a train ride back to Passau.
  - Boats. There are sightseeing boats operating along the Danube River in this area, confirm schedules (times and dates). Recent schedules included boats departing from Passau at 9:00 a.m. and arriving at 12:40 p.m. at Aschach, or returning at 4:15 p.m. from Aschach to Passau at 9:00 p.m. All things being equal, I recommend the morning boat since it moves faster heading down river, and this approach also removes pressure for the ride back since there are no boats to catch.
  - There are also trains along the route, but not near the Danube River, which means taking on more hills and road riding.
- To Aschach, head out of Passau, riding to the southwest along the Danube (be careful to end up on the right river since it is a bit confusing with rivers heading in four directions.)
- At Jochenstein, continue along the eastern side of Danube River, but consider an interesting stop at Engelhartszell and its historic abbey across the river.
- Possible coffee and pastry stop in Obernzell.
- Cross to western side of the river trail by ferry at Schlogen (55 km). At the Donauschlinge Hotel, on the river in Schlogen at the ferry crossing, have a drink, strudel, or one of their fancy ice cream creations. On certain dates a boat operates from Schlogen to Passau (departing 6 p.m. arriving Passau 9 p.m.), or take the morning boat at 9 a.m., arriving at Schlogen at 11:10 a.m., and cycle back.
- Continue to Aschach or Linz as described, with boat and train options for return.

- One more option: This book is all about day riding without moving hotels or carrying much luggage on the bike. As an exception to that approach, consider an overnight in Aschach, carrying only a day bag with one change of off-bike clothes and some necessities, and riding back to Passau the next day. Besides being a great way to address the otherwise somewhat challenging logistics, the other reason for this suggestion is the Hotel Faust Schloss in Aschach, one of my favorites, well-priced, with great views (but a steep driveway), small pool, and special restaurant on a terrace overlooking the Danube.

Ride Along the Danube River toward Aschach   *View from Hotel Faust Schloss in Aschach*

✝ Inn River Ride

- This ride weaves back and forth between Germany and Austria as it takes cyclists south along the Inn River, with options to ride roundtrip to Scharding or Obernberg, or a longer ride to Braunau (about 64 km). Check train schedules before riding if planning a one-way ride. Also, explore sightseeing cruise options on the Inn River, providing a scenic option for your outbound or return journey.
- There are trail options on both sides of the Inn River from Passau, permitting interesting round-trip options. Parts of the trail on some sides is not paved. I also recommend the *Bikeline* map book that details the Inn River ride.

- Passau to Scharding (14.5 km), past the Castle Neuburg and Castle Wernstein, makes a good round-trip destination, providing for 29-km ride on two sides of the river. Scharding is a pleasant small town to explore and have a meal in the town center.
- Scharding to Obernberg (24 km). This makes a good turnaround point for roundtrip ride (77 km total), with trails on both sides of the river for extra variety.
- Obernberg to Braunau (25.5 km). This is a nice tranquil town; hard to believe it was the birthplace of Hitler.
- Slow trains back to Passau for this short distance (1.5 hours), but be sure to check schedules before the ride.

If riding with kids, make sure to stop at the amazing children playground area on the Inn River trail just south of Passau.

Munich Rides

Munich is a vibrant city with much to do, from a walk through its historic center (Alstadt), enjoying a drink or meal at its classic beer gardens, strolling through the former Olympic Village area, or visiting the impressive BMW museum and facilities. There are also many day rides from and around Munich, but here are three that start with a short train ride from Munich to Rosenheim for rides along the Inn River.

RIDE HIGHLIGHTS

+ Ride the Inn River and Lake Chiemsee.

+ Kufstein and Fortress.

+ Visit Schwaz with its memorable silver mine tour.

+ Rattenberg and Wasserburg.

+ **Getting There**: Take the train from Munich central station to Rosenheim (45-minutes) about once an hour.

BMW Museum

Kufstein Castle

RIDE FEATURES

⊞ Hotels:

- These rides involve a 45-minute train each way from Munich to Rosenheim, so consider staying in Rosenheim a couple of nights, though it is not nearly as interesting a destination as Munich. I would suggest that if cycling is your main focus, stay in Rosenheim. If your group includes non-riders or if you want to visit the great spots in Munich when not riding, then stay in Munich.
- If staying in Munich, I recommend staying at one of the many 3-4 star hotels within a few minutes walk of the Munich central train station, known as the Hauptbahnhof. This location facilitates easy use of the trains recommended herein and is also a good location for exploring the city, such as the BMW museum, Olympic village, and the Altstadt.

⊙⊙ Bike Rental:

- Bike rental available at main train station, Radius Tours, Track 32 one of my favorite rental shops in Europe. Ask for Michael, he is a great help (www.radiustours.com).

RIDES

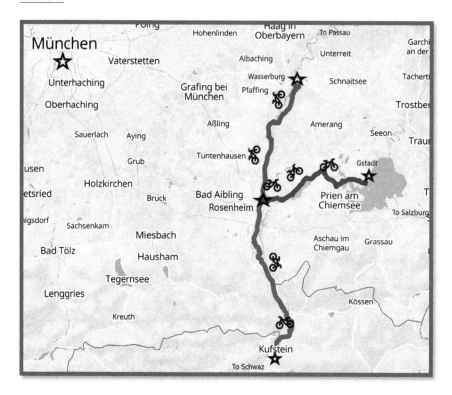

┼ Rosenheim to Wasserburg am Inn Ride

- Train to Rosenheim, and ride on the beautiful (but sometimes not paved) Inn River bike trail north along the west side of the Inn River, to Wasserburg (about 27 km).
- If you stay along the river, there are not many stops, so bring refreshments.
- Enjoy this beautiful town dating to the 12th century, historic center, and walk around the curved riverfront that includes a remarkable outdoor-sculpture display.
- Have lunch, and then ride back to Rosenheim, or train back to Munich (about 1.2 hours back).

✝ Rosenheim to Kufstein or Schwaz Inn River Ride

- Head south on this an enjoyable 35.5-km ride to Kufstein, and return to Rosenheim by bike (71 km), or train back (about 1.2 hours back to Munich).
- There are parts of the ride with trails on both sides of the Inn River, but generally stay on the east side of the river. Some portions are not paved.
- Explore the Kufstein Hohensalzburg Fortress, dating back to the 13th century, and certainly worth a visit. Great views from the top, reached by a funicular railway.

> At the Kufstein Fortress don't miss the fascinating, albeit gruesome, displays about torture and punishment dating to when the fortress served as a prison during the Austro-Hungarian period.

Between Kufstein and Schwaz

- Consider riding further, perhaps to Rattenberg (58 km), an attractive small town known for its glass (Kisslinger Glasswork and plenty of shops), or all the way to Schwaz (about 80 km) but longer train back to Munich (approximately 1.5 hours).

At Schwaz don't miss a memorable tour of the Schwazer Silberbergwerk, a silver mine that dates to the late Middle Ages and once supplied over 85 percent of the world's silver and stood at the heart of Vienna's wealth.

Put on your helmet and provided raincoat and descend into the mine on small trains for a tour of this mine dating back 500 years.

I really liked this tour, and took my 8-year-old son with me -- but not sure all the safety protocols would be approved for a U.S. tour!

⚐ Rosenheim Lake Simssee and Lake Chiemsee Ride

- Lake Chiemsee is known as "The Bavarian Sea" given its large size. (Note that this lake is also discussed in the Salzburg section.)
- There is a long ride from Rosenheim around, and back (96-km round-trip to the lake), but there are also many shorter options.
- Leave Rosenheim heading east and then head up along the bike trail following the west side of the smaller nearby Lake Simssee.
- Follow the bike trail to the larger Lake Chiemsee, which involves handling a couple of hills, through Thalkirchen, Antwort, and Rimsting to the lake.
- Gstadt makes a good destination (28 km) and enjoy the boats available to King Ludwig's Castle at the islands of Herrenchiemsee or take a dip in the lake.
- Return to Rosenheim (56 km) or ride around the lake for a great longer day ride.

✝ Lindau-Lake Bodensee Day rides

- It is about 2.5-hour train ride to Lindau, situated on the eastern side of Lake Bodensee toward Munich, making this a longer but potential day-ride area.
- Please see Lake Bodensee Rides chapter for further details.

✝ Passau Day Rides

- It is just over two-hour train ride to Passau from Munich, where four day rides are recommended in the Passau chapter.

Salzburg Rides

Salzburg is a magical town for a visit, with plenty of castles, museums, beautiful countryside, and cultural events. Now picture *Sound of Music* on a bike -- that's what it's like (sort of) riding along the trails and lakes around Salzburg. There are multiple rides in the mountains and various lakes around Salzburg, some more difficult than others, but here are three day-ride suggestions. These rides can take cyclists around Lake Chiemsee, to the Castle at Burghausen north along the Salzach River, and to Bischofshofen south along the Salzach River, featuring a chance to visit a medieval castle and ice cave.

RIDE HIGHLIGHTS

✦ Ride smaller Salzach River.

✦ Cycle around Chiemsee Lake, largest lake in Bavaria.

✦ Castle at Burghausen.

✦ Ride to Bischofshofen, with the Hohenwerfen Castle and the Eisriesenwelt Ice Caves.

Salzburg and Salzach River

RIDE FEATURES

⊞ Hotels:

- Consider the well-priced (in this expensive city), Motel One Mirabell, though rather institutionally managed and not in the heart of the old town. There are many other choices, and your decision depends how much time you plan to spend at the hotel and your budget.
- For a treat, head for the beautiful Hotel Schloss Leopoldskron, where part of the *Sound of Music* was filmed (the lake scene). About a 15-minute walk from town center.

🚲 Bike Rental:

- Radsport Wagner has a great selection of road and hybrid bikes, as well as e-bikes. Use their website to reserve the model you like ahead (www.radsport-wagner.at).

RIDES

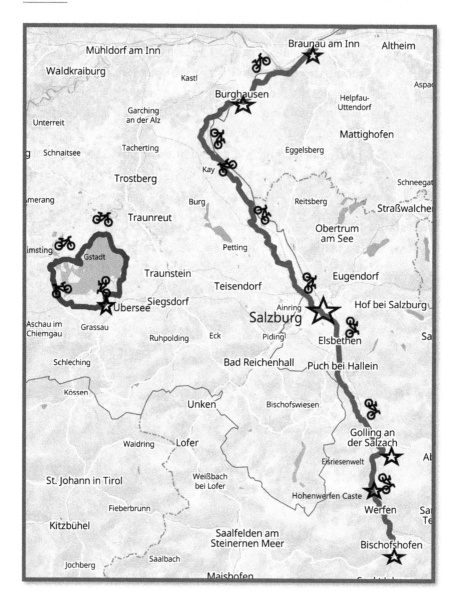

✝ Salzburg to Burghausen Ride

- The ride to the Burghausen Castle is 51.5 km.
- Ride generally north along the Salzach River.
- Visit the incredible Burghausen Castle.

The imposing Burghausen Castle dates back to 1025, and at over 1,000 meters in length it is one of the longest castle complexes in the world. During the period 1255 to 1503, it served as the second residence of the lower Bavarian dukes.

We left our bikes in the lower town and hiked up, taking a couple of hours of walking through the five large courtyards, each originally protected by moats and drawbridges.

- If returning to Salzburg by train, check schedules (can be 2.2 hours with multiple stops).
- Consider the shorter ride to the small town of Oberndorf bei Salzburg (19 km each way).
- If you are looking for more riding from Burghausen continue on the Salzach River, where it soon merges with the Inn River a few kilometers before Braunau (72.5 km total) and then enjoy a 1.5 hour train back (check schedules but easier train connections back from Braunau to Salzburg than from Burghausen).

Along the Salzach River *Chiemsee Lake*

✝ Salzburg to Bischofshofen Ride

- This 53-km ride is generally along the Salzach River and involves a few hills. Consider taking the train there and ride back to Salzburg, especially since you will benefit from a 150-meter decline when riding this direction.
- Make a good stop at Golling an der Salzach at 29 km. Interesting market town to explore and have a snack.
- Consider a stop at the ice caves with stalagmites at Eisriesenwelt and take a hike.
- Continue to the amazing Hohenwerfen Castle, but there is a climb up.
- Ride to Bischofshofen.
- Train ride back (about one hour).

The Hohenwerfen Castle is a medieval rock castle dating back to 1077 built under the Archbishop Gebhard. The castle was damaged by fire over the years, and restored repeatedly. During World War Two it served as a Nazi Education Camp, and then was used by the Austrian rural police force until 1987, when it thankfully became a museum. Several interesting exhibits and tours available.

✝ Lake Chiemsee Ride

- Lake Chiemsee is known as "The Bavarian Sea" given its size in the region. Spend an enjoyable 61-km ride circumnavigating this lake or ride further.
- It is about 50-km ride from Salzburg to Ubersee, a town near Lake Chiemsee, with the route taking riders sometimes on roads and over some hills.
- As an alternative, consider taking a 40-minute train from Salzburg to Ubersee, and use your energy riding around this beautiful lake on flat bike trails and small roads.

- Consider a boat ride to King Ludwig's Castle at the islands of Herrenchiemsee near Gstadt or take a dip in the lake.
- Ride back to Ubersee and train 40 minutes back to Salzburg.
- Another alternative is riding further to Lake Simssee from Rimsting, through Antwort, to Thalkirchen, around the north and then west side of smaller Lake Simssee, and continuing to Rosenheim, where you can train back to Salzburg in about an hour (from Gstadt, it is 28 km to Rosenheim).

Chiemsee and Simsee Lakes Near Rosenheim

Vienna Rides

Vienna has much to offer, from opera to Sacher Torte, but I also recommend two terrific day rides along the Danube River from Vienna, taking riders through the beautiful vineyards and countryside of the Wachau Valley in one direction, or through world-class Roman ruins at Carnuntum and onto Bratislava in Slovakia in the other direction. Vienna is also the perfect place to spend time for non-riders who might not be joining the trip -- make sure you check out the fantastic Museum of Music.

RIDE HIGHLIGHTS

✦ Trails are well-marked, and Bikeline map books are in English.

✦ Most trails stay close to the river, making navigation even easier.

✦ Sightseeing cruise boats are often available that will take bikes along many sections of the Danube.

✦ Beautiful Wachau Valley, Roman Ruins, and Bratislava, nearby.

Beautiful Wachau Valley Ride

Schonbuhel Castle on Danube River

RIDE FEATURES

🏨 Hotels:

- The Austria Classic Hotel Wien is a good choice, near the major train station, well-priced and comfortable rooms (even AC), walking distance to sites, and close to the Danube River trails.

🚲 Bike Rental:

- Vienna Explorer. A large variety of bikes for rent. Also consider their interesting day trips supported with a van and guide to Wachau valley (www.viennaexplorer.com).
- Die Radstation, located at the Hauptbahnhof central station (www.dieradstation.cc).

RIDES

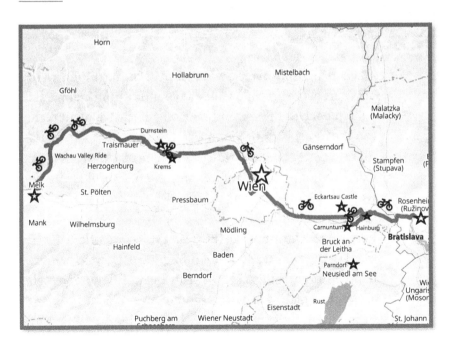

✝ Vienna to Durnstein and the Wachau Valley Ride

- This is a longer ride (88.5 km) just to Durnstein, heading west along the Danube River bike trail.

In the beautiful town of Durnstein make sure to climb to the 12th century ruined castle, the Burgruine Durnstein. The castle sits above the city where Richard the Lionheart was imprisoned (1182-1193) by Leopold V as King Richard was returning from the crusades.

King Richard was finally released after paying a ransom of 150,000 silver marks. The castle was largely destroyed by an explosion orchestrated by the Swedes in 1645.

- After visiting Durnstein, which is near the beginning of the best part of the Wachau Valley as your ride from Vienna, ride 6.5 km back to Krems, and take one of the frequent trains (on the hour) back to Vienna.
- All that being said, the ride from Vienna to Krems is a nice ride, but not nearly as interesting and beautiful as the ride west of Krems along the Danube River, through the heart of the Wachau Valley.
- **Recommendation:** Take the train ride round-trip to Krems to make this a fantastic day of riding. Take the train to Krems in the morning, then ride the truly beautiful route to Melk, along the north side of the Danube River (35 km).
- Climb the hill to visit the world-class Abby at Melk. Have lunch in Melk or in one of the quaint towns between Melk and Durnstein.

- Boats and trains can get you back to Vienna if you have had a long enough ride, or ride back to Krems, making it a 70-km day of riding, and then train back to Vienna. Worth the day!

Melk to Durnstein Beautiful Bike Path

Heidentor Gate

✝ Vienna to Roman Ruins at Carnuntum and Bratislava Ride

- Total ride to Bratislava, Slovakia (67.5 km) with extra riding around the memorable Roman ruins and museum at Carnuntum.
- From Vienna, head across the Danube River over the A23 bridge (Prater Bridge Sudosttangente), then follow the river trail past Schonau and Orth (29 km). The path is mostly paved and straight, often though parklands, with a potential stop at the beautiful Schloss Eckartsau for a visit and coffee.
- Proceed to Hainburg (19 km), cross the river to the south bank, and take a short ride back west to Petronell-Carnuntum.
- If you are interested in ancient history, the Roman ruins at Carnuntum are a must. This was a major Roman outpost along the strategic Danube frontier, and near the battle depicted in the film *Gladiator*! Visit the various ruins by bike, including the Heidentor Gate, the amphitheater, and museum. This is not like visiting Rome, of course, or not even as interesting as Trier for Roman ruins in my opinion, but I truly enjoyed this ride through history, especially being more off the beaten path and visiting the Roman frontier region.

- After the visit head back toward Bratislava to the medieval city of Hainburg, and explore it if you have the time.
- Continue to Bratislava (16 km) from Hainburg.
- Explore the old section of Bratislava, have a great beer and barbeque at the Bratislavky Mestiansky beer garden, then train back to Vienna (one hour, running often).

THE NETHERLANDS

The Netherlands is built around bike riding, with great bike trails almost everywhere, flat terrain, and good route signage. There are more bikes than people in Holland! People take bikes all over, and use them extensively for commuting and shopping, making the urban biking routes particularly crowded at points. Routes are well-marked, with target cities often identified, but there is also the use of a route numbering system. (The *Falk Maps* can be useful in Holland, but not necessary. Useful maps include numbers 11, 12, 13, and 14; www.falk.nl.)

The routes suggested in this book provide riders with a chance to explore historic cities (outside of the crowded Amsterdam), canals, classic sites, and the dunes route along the North Sea. Two base cities are suggested: Amsterdam and Rotterdam, though rather than staying in Amsterdam, consider staying in nearby Haarlem as a base for exploring Amsterdam and riding.

- **Amsterdam/Haarlem** – Explore riding from Amsterdam through the historic and pleasant city of Haarlem, away from the crowds in central Amsterdam. Ride to the North Sea and explore the dunes trail and beaches.

- **Rotterdam** – A terrific city to base several days of riding, including rides to the Dutch capital of The Hague, the beautiful city of Delft, a cheese excursion to Gouda, a classic windmill ride, and a cycle to the Hook of Holland, the mouth of the Rhine River as it flows into the North Sea.

Amsterdam Rides

I actually don't like cycling in central Amsterdam; it's just too crowded, but there are great day ride options nearby. I am suggesting one ride to the interesting city of Haarlem, and onto the North Sea beaches and dune trail -- and even all the way to The Hague.

RIDE HIGHLIGHTS

+ Amazing sites of Amsterdam, including visiting the canals on foot or by tour boat, the Van Gogh Museum, the Rijksmuseum, and the Ann Frank Museum.

+ Short and longer ride options.

+ Riding to the historic and beautiful city of Haarlem.

+ Enjoy a ride along the North Sea route and consider a plunge!

+ Ride all the way to The Hague.

Amsterdam

Bikes in Holland

RIDE FEATURES

🏨 Hotels:

- In Amsterdam, stay at the wonderful Boogaard's Bed & Breakfast. Two rooms with terrific roof deck, so be sure to book ahead. It is friendly, in the middle of the action, yet surprisingly quiet (www.Boogaardsbnb.com).

🚲 Bike Rental:

- There are numerous places to rent a bike in Amsterdam. Great selection at Rent-a-Bike.nl (www.rentabike.nl).
- Another company with wide selection, A-Bike Rental and Tours, which as the name indicates, also offers tours (www.a-bike.nl).

RIDES

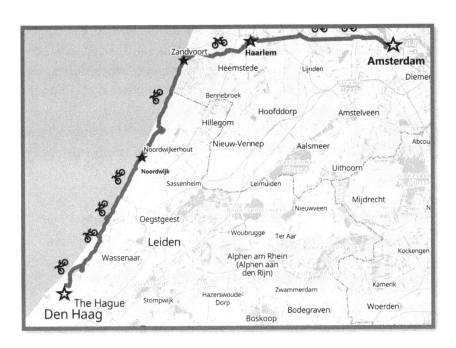

✝ Haarlem and the North Sea Dune Trail

- This route presents a short 19 km-ride to Haarlem, with the option for a train back to Amsterdam, or a round-trip ride. You can also opt for longer rides along the North Sea trail part or all the way to The Hague (67 km).
- There are a couple of routes out of Amsterdam to Haarlem, running generally close together. Follow the bike signs to Haarlem – there are great bike route signs in this area.
  - Head from the central city northwest toward Westerpak near the harbor, then head almost due west along the bike paths near S103 and N200 to Haarlem.
  - Alternatively, head west out of town near the Amsterdam Museum on bike trails to S100 and then S105 to S104 and then into town along the N200.
- From Haarlem, head 6 km to the coastal town of Zandvoort.
- If time permits, head south along the North Sea Dune Bike trail that follows the North Sea all the way to The Hague and beyond. This beautiful, paved bike and hiking trail takes cyclists through parklands, past empty beaches, dunes, and beach towns. This ride reminds me somewhat of riding on Cape Cod or Nantucket Island.
- Zandvoort to The Hague is 42 km or stop at Noordwijk aan Zee (18 km from Zandvoort). The entire ride from Amsterdam to the Hague totals 67 km.

Consider basing your riding from a hotel in Haarlem, an attractive and interesting smaller town that retains its medieval feel dating back to its first walls constructed in 1270.

This historic trading port makes a great base for riding and visiting Amsterdam. Visit the Grote Makt in the center of the city that includes many interesting buildings, the Church of St. Bavo, and the windmill museum at the Molen De Adriaan Museum.

- Train back from The Hague (under 50 minutes) from Haarlem (15 minute train), or from Noordwijk (about 1.2 hours).

Nordwijk Aan Zee on the North Sea Beach   *North Sea Dune Trail*

✝ Additional Rides Options

- See ride options from Rotterdam in the next chapter. Consider enjoying these rides by taking short train rides from Amsterdam to the start and finish of these rides. It is quick and easy to take trains around this part of Holland.
- If you stay in Haarlem, consider one ride to Amsterdam for a day of touring in the city, and the other day ride to the North Sea along the Dune route.

Rotterdam Rides

Rotterdam is far less touristy than Amsterdam, but offers many interesting attractions, and even better day rides. From Rotterdam, try the interesting ride to one of my favorite cities in Holland, the beautiful city of Delft. Delft is a quiet Amsterdam in some ways, the home of Vermeer, small canals, numerous restaurants and cafes, and a fine university. After Delft, visit The Hague, the capital of Holland and home of institutions like the International Court of Justice, and consider a further ride to the North Sea beaches. Taste some local cheese in Gouda, or ride to the end of the Rhine River and see it flow into the North Sea. Finally, no trip to Holland is complete without a classic windmill excursion!

RIDE HIGHLIGHTS

✦ Ride to the end of the Rhine, at the Hook of Holland.

✦ Explore great cities of Delft and The Hague.

✦ Hang out at the North Sea beaches.

✦ Good rail system for quick connections and returns.

✦ Visit historic windmills and the cheese of Gouda.

Hoek Van Holland, the Mouth of the Rhine River   *Bike Route Delft to The Hague*

RIDE FEATURES

囲 Hotels:

- There are many hotels in Rotterdam, but here are two to consider:
- The Ibis Rotterdam City Centre. I generally like the Ibis hotels if you are not planning to spend much time in the room because they are generally clean, efficient, often well-located, and reasonably priced.
- The Rome Mate Bruno Hotel makes a more interesting stay, situated near the river, with some rooms offering attractive water views.

🚲 Bike Rental:

- Zwaan Bikes Rotterdam, with some variety, including e-bikes. No offense to the Dutch, but their bikes tend to be a bit heavy and clunky, so you might need to look around to find something that meets your needs (www.czwaan.nl).

RIDES

✝ Hook of Holland and More Ride

- From Rotterdam, ride west, then northwest, following the Rhine River to where it flows into the North Sea at the Hook of Holland. The ride to the Hook and back to Rotterdam is 29 km each way (58-km round-trip).
- Stop at local seafood restaurants as you approach the Hook.

Spend a few moments at the Kindertransport Holocaust memorial sculpture opened in 2011, near the Hook of Holland. Designed by sculptor Frank Meisler, It is a moving statue commemorating the role played by the Dutch people in helping to save Jewish children fleeing the Holocaust.

- Ride all the way out on the pier that juts out into the North Sea.
- **Grand Ride Option:** Complete an enjoyable loop that takes you to the Hook, then to The Hague, and finally back to Rotterdam through Delft -- all in 74 km!
- Continue the ride along the North Sea bike route to The Hague, following the signs and route northeast (about 21 km). Potential to take train back to Rotterdam (about a 30-minute train ride).
- Even better, continue the ride back from The Hague to Rotterdam, stopping in the beautiful of city of Delft. This route provides 24 km of extra riding from The Hague through Delft to Rotterdam.

✝ The Hague/Delft Ride

- If time permits, rather than adding The Hague to the Hook ride, make it a round-trip ride from Rotterdam to The Hague.
- The route is well-marked. Look for the route signage to lead the way.

- Head west out of Rotterdam and then follow route signs to Delft, past Overschie, Kandelaar, Zweth, then Delft (about 14.5 km).
- Explore Delft, with its classic ceramics, small streets, canals, and museums. Delft might be my favorite city in Holland to explore, so build some time into your ride for a stop.
- Then continue to The Hague, a total of 24 km all the way from Rotterdam -- places are so close together in this part of Holland!
- Consider a short further ride to the beach area of The Hague and spend your afternoon riding along the coast or enjoying the shore.
- For the return to Rotterdam there are a few options: take a short train ride back from The Hague, retrace the route for a round-trip ride, or take an alternative route that is just east of the Rijswikjkse Golf Club near Ypenburg, continuing to Delfgauw (past the IKEA) east of the old city of Delft, toward the Rotterdam airport, passing it to the east, and then to central Rotterdam.

✝ Gouda Ride

- The roundtrip ride to Gouda from Rotterdam is about 48 km and provides two routes: a northerly and southerly route so riders don't have to repeat trails.
- Follow the signs to Gouda, but generally the northern route takes riders to Hillegersberg, Lage Bergs Bos, and then parallel to the A12 into Gouda.
- Explore the charming town of Gouda, especially the amazing cheese shops and exhibits. Of course, Gouda makes an excellent lunch stop.
- Ride back south near the Hollandse Ijssel small river, then near the N219, when the river turns sharply to the southeast (the Eetcafe is a local landmark at this point).

Gouda cheese originated in Holland, and is made from yellow cow's milk giving it a mild flavor.

The town of Gouda was the trading center for this cheese, which dates back to the early 12th century.

This cheese can take as little as a month to age, and is considered very old if aged 12 months or longer.

Come to Gouda and see more cheese than you thought existed on the planet!

⌘ Windmill Route to Kinderdijk Ride

- Visiting windmills is a must for any Dutch riding adventure!
- This is not a long ride, about 16 km each way from central Rotterdam, but a classic route, since the route takes riders along the river to one of the best windmill sites in the world.
- Head east out of Rotterdam along the river and cross the river with the route across the A16 at De Veranda, then continue along the southern side of the river toward Kinderdijk.
- Take the ferry across and explore the windmills and a windmill museum.
- Have lunch and return to Rotterdam for just over a 32-km round-trip ride.

The windmills of Kinderdijk is comprised of 19 large windmills, most built around 1740, and some open for visits. Take a look inside a windmill exhibit and see how the family operators lived.

These giant machines are now a UNESCO World Heritage site. They have been used for centuries to control the waters in Holland and keep the country from flooding.

During your ride also notice the surrounding waterways, dikes, and other features of this complex system.

THE LAKES

Riding around some of the major lakes in Western and Central Europe is a great way to enjoy multiple day rides from a single base location, utilizing the extensive and scenic ferry systems that connect various parts of these lakes. The lakes also combine interesting historic sites, with relaxing beaches, boating, and wildlife in a resort setting. One or two base-town locations permits riding around these entire lakes, and sometimes this can be accomplished from a single base hotel location. All in all, these rides are especially relaxing stops for riders, non-riders, and families.

This book will present three European lakes that offer superb base riding opportunities:

- **Lake Bodensee (Lake Constance) – Germany, Switzerland, Austria** – Just a train ride from Munich, or even Frankfurt or Stuttgart, ride around this beautiful lake, the widening of the Rhine River, visiting up to three countries, and a chance to ride to the spectacular Rhine Falls, Botanic gardens at Mainau Island, historic towns, museums, and more, from one or two base towns.

- **Lake Balaton – Hungary** – A quick train ride from Budapest, experience Hungary at the beach, with easy bike trails, quick access to Budapest, the spa city of Heviz, great ferry network, and a resort feel with a bit of historic settings thrown in.

- **Lake Ferto (Lake Neusiedl) – Hungary, Austria** – Smaller and more limited than the other two lakes, with Austria in the north and Hungary in the south, this lake is a great addition to visits to Vienna, Bratislava, and even Budapest, riding through countryside and with an interconnected ferry system across this relatively shallow body of water.

Lake Bodensee Rides

Lake Bodensee delivers superb, easy day riding, with the option to stay in two different city bases. It provides the opportunity for more than a week of cycling full of charming towns, historic sites, castles, gardens, watersports, and beaching. This lake also makes a good choice for non-riders and families looking to relax together with a rider. The lake is basically the widening of the Rhine River, as it makes it way down from the Alps, bulging at the lake, then narrowing radically as it makes its way past the impressive Rhine Falls to Basel. From there it becomes the grand navigable Rhine River that flows to Rotterdam and the North Sea. There are many attractive towns to stay in, but I am recommending two in particular: Lindau (convenient train ride to Munich), and Konstanz (larger, more diverse, town on the lake), as bases for day rides. It is easy to spend a week at Lake Bodensee enjoying the atmosphere and days of riding!

RIDE HIGHLIGHTS

+ Three countries in a week! Germany, Switzerland, and Austria.

+ Easy touring, well-marked trails -- family and child friendly.

+ Vacation atmosphere with beaches, boats, and holiday hotels. Consider making hotel reservations for this trip June-September – this time of year can be relatively crowded.

+ Third largest lake in Central Europe (540 square km), just a bit smaller than Lake Geneva and Lake Balaton in Hungary. Formed during last Ice Age through the Rhine Glacier.

+ Numerous cities and sites with over 270 km of paved, hard packed, and small road trails.

+ Ferry and Rail system allows riders to move around the Lake.

+ **Getting There**: Train from Munich to Lindau (about 3 hours) and ferry or local train to location. Longer train from Frankfurt or 1.5 hours train ride from Zurich.

View from Deck at Viva Sky Hotel in Konstanz   *Ferry System Around the Lake*

RIDE FEATURES

⌂ Hotels:

- **Konstanz.** There are many fine hotels in Konstanz, but consider the Viva Sky Hotel, which offers terrific views and rooftop restaurant and bar. A good Indian restaurant is located right across street.
- **Lindau.** Consider the upscale Hotel Bad Schachen a bit out of town, for a resort feel, with pool, on the lake. Another option is staying in the central town, such as the Boutique-Hotel Adara (3.5 stars).

🚲 Bike Rental:

There are many bike rental opportunities around the lake, but here are some suggestions:

- **Konstanz**
  - Landenbach offers a wide variety of bikes. (www.landenbach-konstanz.de).
  - Fahrradeck (www.fahrradeck-konstanz.de).
- **Lindau**
  - Fahrrad Unger (www.fahrrad-unger.de).
  - Jausovec (www.radsport-jausovec.de).

RIDES

Before starting the rides, find schedules and routes of ferries and trains operating during your trip, and use them as a transportation network around the lake. They provide great opportunities to skip sections or complete longer one-way trips.

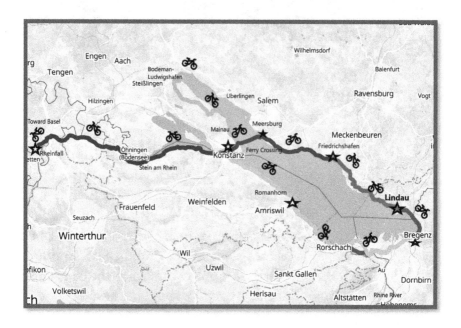

✝ North Side: Lindau to Meersburg Ride

- Ride along the north side of the lake on the bike trail to Meersburg (about 53 km).
- Explore a castle along the route, the Schloss Montfort.
- Further along, before Meersburg, enter Friedrichshafen (25.5 km), with a strong recommendation to visit the Zeppelin Museum. Friedrichshafen is not an attractive town, given it was mostly destroyed in World War Two because of its strategic industrial base.

 The Zeppelin Museum contains the world's largest airship collection related to the Zeppelin airships, opened in 1996. We most enjoyed the exhibits on the ill-fated Hindenburg, including recreated cabins, as well as the history of airships and balloons.

A great place to spend a couple hours, including with families. Outside there is a terrific zeppelin playground.

- Consider a round-trip from Lindau to Friedrichshafen and back, for a 51-km total ride.
- If continuing to Meersburg, one of the most attractive towns on the lake and well-worth a visit, train back to Friedrichshafen and ride back to Lindau, or take ferries, potentially through Konstanz.

✝ South Side: Lindau to Romanshorn (Switzerland) Ride

- Ride south along the lake path, south and then west, to Romanshorn (35 km one-way or 70-km roundtrip).
- Leaving Lindau ride to Bregenz, Austria (10 km). Consider the Pfanderbahn cable car ride and fantastic view.
- Continue on the bike trail to Gaissau (17.5 km) riding over the Rhine River inlet where the Rhine River descends from the Alps and enters the lake.
- Ride further to Romanshorn (14.5 km).
- Return to Lindau by ferry or make it a round-trip ride.

✝ Konstanz to Meersburg Ride

- This 78-km route is a terrific ride, but the section between Bodman to Konstanz was washed out the last time I did the ride (check status when you go). It might be necessary to ride on various roads, some hilly, and with limited traffic through this segment. Use ferries to avoid this stretch, taking the ferries to Ludwigshafen from Konstanz.

- As discussed above, Meersburg is one of my favorite towns on the lake.
- Stop at Mainau Island and its beautiful gardens.

✝ Konstanz to Friedrichshafen Meersburg Ride

- Take a ferry from Konstanz to Meersburg.
- Explore this attractive town.
- Head on the bike trial to Friedrichshafen (19 km one way). Enjoy the small resort towns and countryside along this route.
- Visit the Zeppelin Museum as discussed above.
- Take ferry back to Konstanz from Friedrichshafen or ride back to Meersburg for beautiful 38 km round-trip ride.

Riding Along the Lake Near Uberlingen

Riding to Rhine Falls

✝ Konstanz to Bregenz Ride

- This 72-km ride takes riders out of the German town Konstanz riding through Switzerland, to the Austrian town of Bregenz (72 km). You can visit three countries in a day!
- Most of the ride is along good bike path, easier and generally better than German north side of lake, but less interesting and scenic.
- The Pfanderbahn cable-car ride in Bregenz is recommended, consider walking one-way if so inclined!
- Only 10 km further to Lindau if you like, and longer ferry back, but be sure to check schedules before the ride.

✝ Konstanz to Rhine Falls Ride

- This 51.5-km ride takes riders to the Rhine Falls -- a fantastic stop I highly recommend. Hike down the falls trail for a closer look, and even consider a boat ride for an up close and personal look! These are my favorite falls in Western Europe.
- Head south out of Konstanz and the follow the Rhine River west toward Stein Am Rhine.
- Continue along generally near the river or parallel to it, to Schaffhausen. You are only 4 km to the Rhine Falls.
- Ride back, train back, or take mid-afternoon boat back to Konstanz (confirm it is operating and times).

Rhine River Falls at Schaffhausen   *Giant Flower at Mainau Island Gardens*

The Mainau Island is a 45 hectare park and gardens that makes a beautiful stop, especially great for families. Stroll through natural gardens, flowers of every types, the butterfly house, and sculptured hedges. Each season brings something special to this island.

✝ Short Ride Option: Konstanz to Mainau Island Ride

- This is a short 6 km ride each way, great for kids and for short-distant riders.
- Visit the beautiful 45-hectare Mainau Island Attraction, which includes large botanic gardens, a palace, butterfly center, restaurants, and amazing kids play area. Two-hours-plus should be allocated (www.mainau.de).
- Note: You ride past Mainau Island on the way to Meersburg, so this visit can be combined with that ride or as a round-trip from Konstanz.

Lake Balaton Rides

Lake Balaton, the largest lake in Central Europe, is a wonderful place to spend multiple days riding and exploring, with bike trails that circumvent the lake (totaling about 195 km around). Bike trails exist on all sides of the lake, but I prefer riding along the south side, which is a bit quieter and less hilly. The lake offers many additional attractions: swimming, boating, historic and modern towns, local fairs, and the spa city of Heviz. Ferry boats and trains connect various locations, providing for many one-way riding opportunities. As is the case with Lake Bodensee, one could decide to stay in two locations, at different ends of the lake, such as Keszthely and Siofok, perhaps. However, I am going to suggest staying in one small, centrally located, moderately-priced resort hotel and use that as your base.

RIDE HIGHLIGHTS

+ Relatively low-cost for a resort area.

+ Great multifeatured vacation area.

+ A special dip at the incredible spa lake at Heviz.

+ Great ferry infrastructure (www.balatonihajozas.hu).

+ **Getting There**. Take a train from the Budapest-Deli station to Balatonboglar (target hotel location) in under 2 hours (non-stop, operating often).

Lake Balaton *PartVilla Hotel Beach*

RIDE FEATURES

🏨 Hotels:

- Consider a stay at the wonderful PartVilla in Balatonboglar. About 25 rooms dating back to 1932, directly on the lake with a small beach, beach bar, restaurant, and boat rentals. This serves as a central location for days of riding and a low-key resort to stay and enjoy.

🚲 Bike Rental:

- Rent a bike in Budapest and take it with you so that you can insure the highest quality and type you want, with bikes from Thomas Radil, who runs Bike and Relax, a good choice (www.bike-and-relax.com). He can also help with logistics for additional riding or even transport.
- Bikes are available at the PartVilla, but they might not be of the highest quality. There are also rentals available nearby at Fredo Tourists (www.fredotoursit.hu).

RIDES

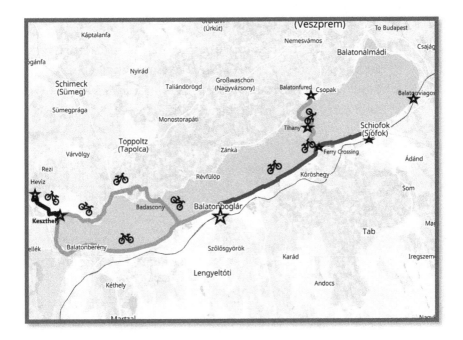

☦ Balatonboglar to Keszthely.

- Head west from the hotel and follow the lake path (40 km) to Keszthely.

- Keszthely might be the most interesting city on the lake, and worth a couple hours of exploring. The Festetics Castle, dating back to 1754, is an especially attractive stop, even if you don't go in and just cycle around the various gardens. The central market street in town is also worth a stroll.

- Various options from here: Ride back, take a ferry back (one hour), take a 40-minute train back, or continue the ride around the north side of the lake and take the ferry boat back from various towns: Balatongyorok (9 km), Szigliget (an additional 11 km), or Badacsony (an additional 8 km from Szigliget), but expect some hills.

✝ Balatonboglar to Heviz Ride

- Ride to Keszthely (40 km).
- Head to Heviz (an additional 7 km) with some hills.
- For a special treat enjoy a plunge in the large thermal lake and swimming complex at the Heviz Healing Lake.
- Ride back to Keszthely, and train, bike, or ferry back (one hour ferry ride is my first choice!).

At the lake in Heviz, wade into the medicinal waters in a way you have never experienced! The lake contains a mixture of sulfur, calcium, magnesium, hydrogen carbonate, and more that reportedly can address a variety of ailments.

We enjoyed the warm water, swimming across the waters in this large complex tailor made to compliment a bike ride! There is a charge to enter, but it is a worthwhile experience. For a free swim in similar water, look for the small stream just upstream where many are bathing free of charge.

✝ Balatonboglar to Tihany Ride

- Ride east along the lake trail and take the ferry across to Tihany (29 km).
- Explore the area, including the Benedictine Abby of Tihany. There is a hill climb involved, not trivial, but worthwhile.
- Consider riding further to Balatonfured (about 9 km) and taking long ferry back (2.5 hours).

The Benedictine Abby of Tihany was founded in 1055, and the current church dates back to 1754. King Andrew was buried here in 1060, and is the only medieval King of Hungary remaining in a preserved crypt.

- Otherwise, ride back from Tihany (less than 64 km total), take two-hour ferry back from Tihany, or train back from locations on the south shore such as Balatonfoldvar (20 minutes, every hour).

Festetics Castle in Keszthely   *Ferry Ride Lake Balaton Near Tahany*

✝ Balatonboglar to Siofok Ride
- Ride northeast along the lake to Siofok (35 km).
- Have a snack or meal and enjoy the town. Ride or train back.
- Consider taking a ferry to Balatonfured, then riding back through Tihany on way back to Balatonboglar or continuing along the more hilling north side of the lake to Revfulop (27 km from Balatonfured) for a 40-minute ferry ride back.

Lake Ferto/Neusiedl Lake Rides

Lake Neusiedl, as it is called in Austria (the majority and northern part of the lake) and Lake Ferto, its name in Hungary (the southern part of the lake) is the largest endorheic lake (generally retains water without drainage to rivers or oceans) in Central Europe. The lake is attractive and well worth the visit, but rather shallow and can look a bit muddy (at least during my visit). There is plenty of enjoyable riding, but not in the same league as Lake Bodensee or Lake Balaton as far as diversity and scenery. Around the lake I have suggested four day rides on small roads and bike paths, through wetlands, past small resort towns, and with some climbs as you pedal through an area that played an important role in the fall of East Germany. After the border crossing climb to the wonderful city of Sopron in Hungary.

RIDE HIGHLIGHTS

+ Up to four days of beautiful rural riding.
+ Combination of bike trials and small roads with easy navigation.
+ Resort towns, wetlands, ferries.
+ Historical town of Sopron and the Pan-European Picnic, which was the beginning of the end of the Berlin Wall.
+ Experience both Austria and Hungary on a bike.
+ **Getting There:** Easy short train rides from Bratislava and Vienna.

Bike Path Near Lake Ferto

RIDE FEATURES

▦ Hotels:

- Consider staying in Hotel am See in Rust, with some rooms with great lake views.
- In Sopron, I really like the 19th-century Pannonia Hotel, which is well-priced, with beautiful two-story dining room, great staff, pool and spa. Located a few blocks from the train station, which makes it convenient for walking around the old city (www.pannoniahotel.com).

🚲 Bike Rental:

- Rent a bike in Vienna or Bratislava if coming from one of those cities, perhaps from a bike rental shop recommended in the chapters about day rides from those cities.
- On the lake, there are bike rental shops in different locations. For example, from Rust, Migschitz provides a selection of rentals (www.migschitz.at).
- On the other side of the lake in Podersdorf, consider the well-named Mike's Radverleih for rentals and tours, including recommended downloadable cycle maps of the lake (www.mikes-bikes.at).

RIDES

The cycle path around the lake totals 120 km and can be divided based on the time you have available. Staying in Rust, Podersdorf, and Sopron are all recommended. Sopron is one of my favorite towns in Hungary, less travelled (have you heard of it before?), with an interesting medieval core and museums. But it is up a hill, so getting there from the lake requires climbing, which might not make it as convenient for multiple days of riding. The following are suggestions for rides if staying in the lakefront resort town of Rust, which is my recommended hotel location on the lake.

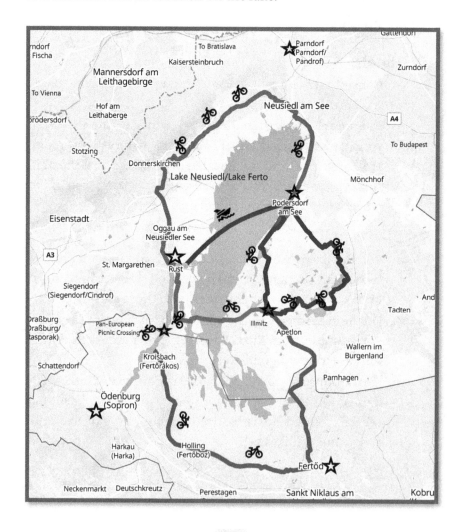

✝ South Loop Ride.

- From Rust ride 35 km south along the lake to Fertod (Hungary), where you can visit the Eszterhaza Palace dating from 1760.
- Then ride north 32 km though wetlands and scenic trails to Podersdorf, then ferry back to Rust (total 72 km).

✝ North Loop Ride.

- From Rust ride north around the lake to Neusiedl am See on this 75-km ride, then head south head south to Podersdorf and then to Illimitz.
- Then head back to the lake and ferry to Morbisch.
- Ride north back to Rust.

✝ Eastern Shore Ride.

- This 55-km ride involves a ferry trip from Rust to Pordersdorf, and then heading south along the lake trail to Illimitz (Hungary).
- Head generally east on a zig-zag bike trail that goes past the south side of several small lakes (Darscho, Lange Lacke, Zicksee), then head northwest back to Podersdorf and ferry back to Rust (55 km).

Before reaching Sopron we pedaled across a historic Austrian-Hungarian border that was the site of the Pan-European Picnic. This Picnic was a peaceful demonstration that took place in August 1989, when the border gate between the countries was opened.

Many attribute this as an important moment in the fall of the Berlin Wall and the reunification of Germany. Visit the interesting museum on the subject in Sopron.

✝ Sopron Ride.

- This 36-km ride is an historic trek, riding south from Rust, crossing the famous Austrian-Hungarian border south of Morbisch, and then climb some hills to Sopron near Fertorakos.
- Sopron is a relatively undiscovered city with a medieval core, old churches, and two very old synagogues that are being renovated during my last visit. It is situated above the lake and it takes some climbing to reach the city center, but is certainly one of my favorite stops in Hungary.
- Ride back to Rust.

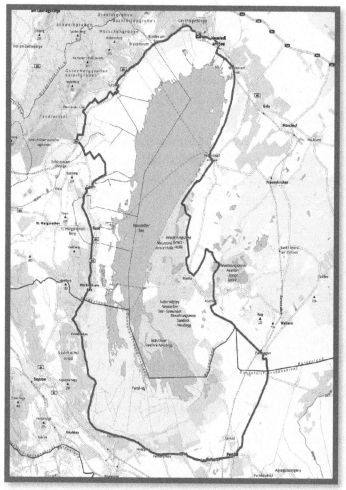

Map of Lake Neusiedl

HUNGARY, CZECH REPUBLIC, AND SLOVAKIA

Grouped in Central Europe, the cities of Budapest, Prague, and Bratislava make for exciting visits and sightseeing. But short rides out of these cities gives an entirely different experience, away from the crowds, often quickly taking riders through small villages, past historic ruins, and to castles that harken to the past.

- **Budapest** – Budapest is a fascinating city to visit, but very different from the rest of Hungary. Enjoy a ride out of town along the Danube to smaller Hungarian towns and rural areas, and consider a trip to Lake Balaton, the largest lake in Central Europe (discussed in the lake section of the book).

- **Prague** – Prague hosts amazing sites and offers so much to do, but the ride on the Vltava and Elbe Rivers to Melnik and the concentration camp of Terezin is worth the time. Other rides whisk you to historic castles and give you a taste of the famous Greenway Trail Bike Route that connects Prague and Vienna.

- **Bratislava** – Bratislava is the capital of Slovakia and is becoming a more significant tourist destination, especially for European tourist. One ride is a first-class adventure along the Danube River to Roman ruins, castles, and even to Vienna. The second ride crosses the border into Hungary and to the lesser-known Hungarian city of Gyor, gliding through the Hungarian countryside. Also consider a trip to nearby Lake Neusiedl (discussed in the lake section of the book).

Budapest Rides

Budapest is an amazing city to explore, and a fun city to bike around (during my last visit we did a night riding tour around town with Thomas Radil, mentioned under the bike rental section). I am recommending two rides out of town. One takes riders west along the Danube, through the Budapest suburbs and then to the charming riverfront village of Szentendre and beyond. The other ride involves a short train ride to Lake Balaton and a day of riding around the lake.

RIDE HIGHLIGHTS

✦ Once outside of Budapest, enjoy lower cost than many other locations in Europe.

✦ Variety of Danube River towns and Lake Balaton.

✦ Visit quiet Hungarian towns, villages, and castles.

Budapest

Szentendre

RIDE FEATURES

🏨 Hotels:

- There are many hotel options in Budapest, but if you find a good price, consider a special night at the centrally located Intercontinental Hotel Budapest and ask for a room with amazing river views. We had the curtains open all night and breakfast in our room enjoying our great view every morning!

🚲 Bike Rental:

- Thomas Radil runs Bike and Relax in Budapest with good bike rentals and local riding information and support options (www.bike-and-relax.com).

Bike Path Along Danube near Szentendre *Signage from Budapest to Szentendre Route*

RIDES

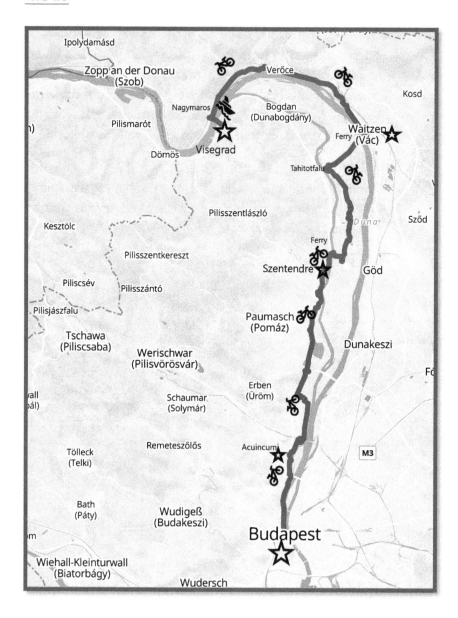

✝ Budapest Along the Danube Ride.

- The Danube River flows through the core of Budapest, separating its two majestic halves. It practically calls out for a bike ride. Take up the call and ride north back toward Bratislava and enjoy a taste of a longer Danube River cycle tour.

- First, head north on the west side of the Danube to Szentendre, an attractive small town requiring only 24 km of pedaling. The first section of the ride is through Budapest's suburbs, not that scenic, but interesting. The ride continues past attractive river houses, and finally opens up to more rural scenery as you proceed further from Budapest.

- Stay on the trail along the Danube River (even if the route takes you along a busier road). Stop for a quick look at the Roman Ruins at Aquincum along the way.

- Szentendre is a charming, though discovered, small town. Enjoy the shops and stroll around quiet streets. I recommend a coffee, drink, or meal at one of the riverfront cafes. We had a great breakfast here last trip after an early start from Budapest.

- Consider a roundtrip ride back to Budapest (48 km).

- Note that there are boats that operate back to Budapest from Szentendre, as well as from the next stop at Vac, and this makes a wonderful way to complete a round-trip (ride out, boat back). Check schedules and confirm bikes are accepted (which they normally are). For example, one boat company to look at is the MAHART PassNave Line.

- I recommend continuing north out of town along the Danube River and crossing over to the adjacent island by ferry toward Szigetmonstor, just past Szentendre, then proceeding on the roadway with low-to-moderate traffic to Tahitotfalu (13.5 km).

- Ride northeast then to Vac (about 3 km) and take a ferry to Vac. Explore the interesting town of Vac. There is a fast 41-minute train back to Budapest from Vac, or ride round-trip ride, or continue further to worthwhile town of Visegrad (another 17 km).
- At Visegrad cross the river by ferry at Nagymaros (57.5 km total ride).
- Climb to the Visegrad Castle for a terrific view and interesting visit, or take bus or taxi up to the viewpoints.

The Visegrad Castle was first built in 1250, and expanded many times over the centuries, though severely damaged during Turkish times. Most modern rebuilding started in the late 19th century.

View from Visegrad Castle

We took the city bus up to the castle rather than attempt the hard climb, leaving our bikes locked near the public visitor center close to the river. We enjoyed the various exhibits, but the best part was the view of the river valley we had just explored by bike.

- Take a 40-minute train ride back to Budapest or consider a beautiful cruise one-way. Check on boat schedules before your ride. For example, there is a 6:00 p.m. boat that often sails back to Budapest. Confirm bikes are accepted. Taking a morning boat from Budapest to Visegrad can also work, giving you the entire day to bike back to Budapest without concern for boat schedules.

Ferry to Vac   *Triumphal Arch in Vac*

✝ Lake Balaton Day Ride

- I suggest several days of riding around Lake Balaton in the lake section of this book. As an alternative, if you are looking for only a day ride from Budapest, take an early morning train with your bike to Lake Balaton.
- Ride length can vary, from 24 km to 50 km for suggested loops, but longer options are easy to find if that is your objective.
- There are many riding options around the lake, but here is one plan: Train from Budapest to Siofok (about 1.2-hour train ride from Budapest). For an extra 11 km of riding along the lake, get off the train at Balatonvilagos, and ride toward Siofok.
- From Siofok, ride to Szantod, and take a ferry over to the island of Tihany, and explore, including climbing to the Benedictine Abby of Tihany, founded in 1055, with a current church dating to 1754 -- worth the climb for the view alone (16 km from Siofok).
- Then head to Balatonfured, about 8 km to the train station, for train back to Budapest (2 hours). If you want more riding, continue to Balatonalmadi (an additional 15 km) then train to Budapest (1.8 hours).

Bratislava Rides

Bratislava has changed dramatically over the last decade, increasingly becoming a tourist destination. It is also an easy addition to a trip to Vienna, Budapest, or Prague. Here are three suggested day rides: a ride along the Danube to the Roman ruins and attractions of Carnuntum, a ride through the Hungarian countryside to the city of Gyor, and a day ride at Lake Neusiedl/Ferto.

RIDE HIGHLIGHTS

✦ Offering a variety of different types of rides.

✦ Rides in three countries: Austria, Slovakia, Hungary.

✦ Terrific Roman ruins and history, the less-developed Hungarian countryside, and a lake connecting Austria and Hungary.

✦ **Getting There:** Easy train rides from Vienna, Budapest, and Prague.

Riding toward Carnuntum

Approaching Bratislava from Hainburg Along Trail

RIDE FEATURES

🏨 Hotels:

- Consider staying at one of the boat hotels on the Danube River, or even the well-priced (sometimes) larger Radisson Blu Carlton, near the Danube River and town center.
- Highly recommended: the Bratislavky Mestiansky classic beer garden.

🚲 Bike Rental:

- Procycling. Nice selection including e-bikes (www.procyclingrental.com)
- Bike Bratislava (www.bikebratislava.sk).

RIDES

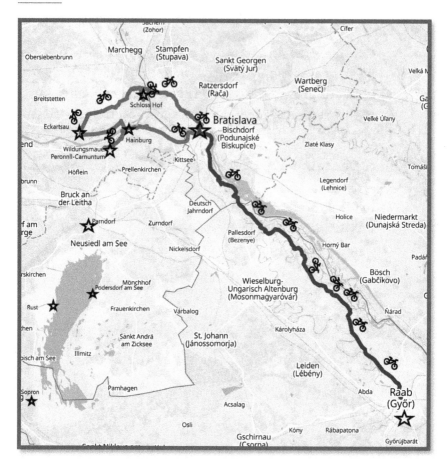

☩ Roman and Castle Danube River Grand Loop Ride

- This route takes riders to the Roman ruins of Carnuntum, and then to two castles on the north side of the Danube River on the way back to Bratislava. Round-trip just to Carnuntum is 45 km, and full route is 90 km. A really terrific ride!

- From Bratislava, cross to the south side of the Danube, over the large central bridge, and head on the bike trail west to Hainburg, sometimes along Route B9 (16 km).

- Explore the medieval city of Hainburg.

- If you are interested in ancient history, the Roman ruins at Carnuntum are a must.

Carnuntum was a major Roman outpost along the strategic Danube frontier, and near the location of the battle involving Marcus Aurelius depicted in the film *Gladiator*.

It was the headquarters of the Pannonian fleet about 50 AD, and became a city of almost 50,000 inhabitants. The historic area is almost 10 square km in size, so visiting by bike is perfect.

Ride dusty unpaved roads and through fields to discover different ruins, such as the Heidentor Gate. Visit various other sites, including an amphitheater that sometimes hosts plays and other events, and a museum. This is not like going to Rome, but it is worth the exploration!

- Ride back toward Hainburg, and cross the Danube at Bad Deutsch-Altenburg, and then head west along the part bike trail about 6.5 km to the Schloss Eckartsau castle for a visit and coffee.
- At this point, the easiest route is retracing the riding route back over the bridge and east to Bratislava.
- However, I recommend a 15-km ride to the Schloss Hof on your return, riding toward Kopfstetten, Loimersdorf, and Engelhartstetten on small roads to the Schloss Hof castle and its wonderful gardens.

The Schloss Hof is an imperial palace worth a visit, located in Austria near the Slovakian border. It was built in the early 18th century as the country estate for Prince Eugene. The palace and gardens now occupy 120 acres for exploration, including a petting zoo.

- Ride 17 km back to Bratislava, heading east to Devinska Nova Ves over the Morava River, to Dubravka and then Bratislava. Note that much of this extra ride north of the Danube is on small roads, not dedicated bike trails.

I grew up in Chicago and really like barbeque ribs. I have to say that the ribs at the Bratislavky Mestiansky beer garden were among my favorite!

✝ Lake Ferto/Neusiedl Lake Ride

- Chose to ride through small roads and some cycle paths 35 km southwest from Bratislava to Neusiedl am See, and start your lake riding there, or take the short train ride to Parndorf from Bratislava and spend the day exploring the lake.
- Enjoy a loop ride (Rust-Pordersdorf-Parndorf) around part of the lake (with ferry connection is 42 km). Add the roundtrip from Bratislava and the total ride is up to 112 km.

Rust in Lake Ferto / Neusiedl *Ferry Crossing Lake Neusiedl*

- For this mini-circumnavigation, ride along the west side of the lake to Rust (about 24 km), which is a nice spot for a snack or lunch.

- Take a scenic ferry crossing to Pordersdorf am See, and head north along the east side of the lake and ride to Parndorf (18 km) for train back to Bratislava, or ride back to Bratislava if you are looking for a long day.

Entering Hainburg *Beautiful City of Gyor*

☨ Hungarian Countryside to Gyor Ride.

- This 80-km ride is through quiet rural Hungarian areas, parts of Hungary that were near the former Cold War border with the west. This is a chance to see the quieter sections of Hungary that most miss when only visiting Budapest.
- More than half of this ride is on smaller roads, not bike trails, and most of the ride is not along the Danube River. I suggest the *Bikeline* map guide, or a good map or GPS, for this ride, since it is generally not on routed pathway. Bring cash for this ride since fewer credit cards are accepted on this route than on others. Cross the Danube River at Bratislava, and head south along the Danube toward Rusovce, Cunovo, Dunakiliti, Dunasziget, Puski, Lipot (consider a dip in the spa lake complex), Asvanyraro, Dunaszeg, and then onto Gyor.
- Spend at least an hour or two exploring Gyor, one of my favorite stops in Hungary, with its historic center and open market, churches, and former synagogue (converted into a general museum).
- Take the two-hour train ride back to Bratislava.

Prague Rides

Prague is an incredible city to explore and enjoy. I could write an entire book on the amount to see and visit, but let's focus on the biking. This section contains four proposed day rides: along rivers, sampling the Greenway trail, to castles, past charming cities, and to the infamous concentration camp at Terezin.

RIDE HIGHLIGHTS

✦ Sample the Prague to Vienna Greenway bike trail.

✦ Visit the castles at Karlstejn and Konopiste.

✦ Ride along river routes and through small towns, sampling Czech brew.

✦ Visit the notorious Terezin Concentration camp and exhibit.

Prague

Convergence of Vltava and Elbe River at Melnik

RIDE FEATURES

🏨 Hotels:

- There are many amazing hotels in Prague, but consider the Grand Majestic Hotel Prague or the Bishop's House, if they are offering attractive pricing for your dates.

🚲 Bike Rental:

- Praha Bike. Very good selection, and great local knowledge of local bike routes. Also consider joining them for one of their interesting organized and supported day ride tours (www.Prahabike.cz/rentals).

RIDES

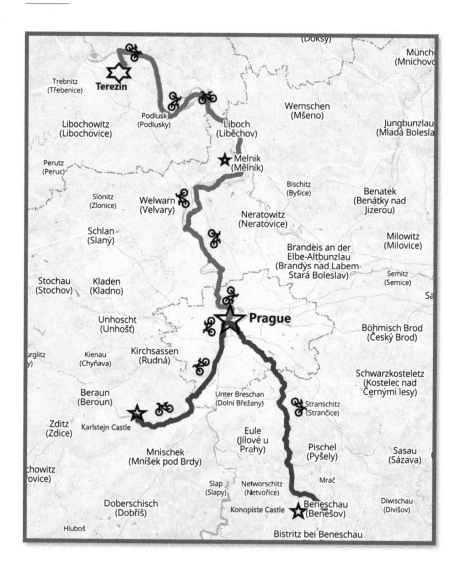

✝ Prague to Melnik/Terezin Ride

- This long 103-km ride along the Vltava and Elbe Rivers to Terezin offers good variety and is generally flat with only one notable climb.

- Cross the Vltava River at Prague and head north along the east side of the river. Considerable portions of this route are not paved or are along quiet roadways.

- There are a few small towns to stop at along this route including Kralupy (at 29 km) and Melnik (an additional 26 km).

- Enjoy exploring Melnik, at the confluence of the Elbe and Vltava Rivers, and sample the local wine. After this 51-km ride, consider opting for a one-hour train ride back to Prague.

- Ride another 48 km to the Nazi concentration camp of Terezin, outside of Litomerice.

Allow a few hours for a moving visit of Terezin. The camp was organized in 1940, as part of a Nazi propaganda program to show the world that things were not that bad in the camps, and was portrayed as a harmless self-governed Jewish settlement area.

Over 150,000 Jews, including 15,000 children, were sent to the camp, and 33,000 died here at the hands of the Gestapo. Before being used as a concentration camp, Terezin was a military fortress dating to the late 18th century.

- Ride back to Lovosice for 1.2-hour direct train back to Prague, or train from Litomerice with a train change.

- For a shorter ride, consider taking a morning train to Melnik and then ride to Terezin, followed by a train back to Prague. (48 km.)

✝ Konopiste Castle and Sample the Greenway Ride

- The famous Greenway Cycle Route between Prague and Vienna is between 350-420 km long (depending on route selections) and makes for a splendid extended riding tour.
- But for a day ride, consider a shorter ride along this route to the Konopiste Castle (65 km) with some hills. This is a beautiful ride through the Czech countryside, providing plenty of opportunities to sample local beers.
- Arrive at the castle and enjoy a tour.

The Konopiste Castle dates back to the 13th century, and was the last residence of the Archduke Franz Ferdinand of Austria, whose assassination on June 28, 2014, triggered World War One. The castle is designed like a typical French fortress with cylindrical towers, watchtower, four gates, and a drawbridge.

- Obtain a detailed route map for this section of the Greenway to best support your ride.
- Less than an hour train ride back from nearby Benesov.

Approaching Melnik

Litomerice, Near Former Terezin Ghetto

✝ Karlstejn Castle Route

- This 35-km route takes riders along a flat bike trail from Prague to the Karlstejn Castle as well as along two rivers. About 10 percent of the ride is along roads.
- Head south along the Vltava River until it splits to the Berounka River, and follow the Berounka River route past Cernosice to Karlstejn.

Karlstejn Castle was founded in 1348, by King Charles IV, the King of Bohemia and the Holy Roman Emperor-elect. The castle served as the safekeeping place for the imperial jewels until 1420. Karlstejn is the most visited castle in the Czech Republic, with over 200,000 visitors annually.

- Consider time for a one-hour tour of this imposing castle, including the interior.
- Return by bike for a longer ride, or return to Prague on a 40-minute train ride.

ITALY

The region of Northern Italy between Lake Garda and Venice offers especially attractive and relatively flat day-ride opportunities. Visit the breathtaking Lake Garda, the historic city of Verona, the less-visited but fascinating cities of Vicenza and Padua, and leave the crowds of Venice to explore the surrounds and the greater lagoon area. Florence, further south, also offers beautiful, albeit hillier, day rides.

- **Verona** – Verona offers ancient, medieval and Renaissance attractions all packed into one location, and serves as a convenient base for terrific rides to Lake Garda, along the Adige River, and along the Mincio River to Mantova.

- **Padua** – Padua is packed with history, art, and a fascinating botanic garden, and is one of my favorite cities in Italy that so few have visited. It is close to Venice, but with a very different feel. Explore the Vento countryside riding to Vicenza or to the seaside town of Chioggia, south of Venice.

- **Venice** – Venice is an amazing place that justifies the crowds, but a short ferry ride across the lagoon is the town of Lido – straddling the lagoon and the Adriatic Sea -- and from there, day rides are available down the barrier islands and around the countryside surrounding Venice.

- **Florence** – Tuscany with its hills and vineyards is hard to beat. Try some rides through the hilly countryside, and even consider an adventurous ride to Siena by bike.

Verona Rides

Verona is a fantastic city to spend several days enjoying and exploring history, food, and culture. While you are there, consider these four proposed day rides: to beautiful Lake Garda, rides around the lake, a cycling exploration of the Vento to Vicenza with its amazing architecture by Andrea Palladio, and finally a ride to the town of Mantova following a river flowing south from Lake Garda.

RIDE HIGHLIGHTS

✦ A variety of rides and experiences.

✦ Great food and, of course, Gelato!

✦ Attractions, history, and architecture.

✦ **Getting There:** Take a train from Venice, Florence, or Milan.

Verona Roman Arena   *Lake Garda*

RIDE FEATURES

🏨 Hotels:
- The Grand Hotel des Arts provides a good breakfast and is a short walk to town or the train station. Friendly staff.

🚲 Bike Rental:
- Verona Bike Rental has a good selection of bikes, including road bikes and e-bikes. The shop is quite experienced in the region and can give you insights and local knowledge about routes (www.gardabikerental.it).

RIDES

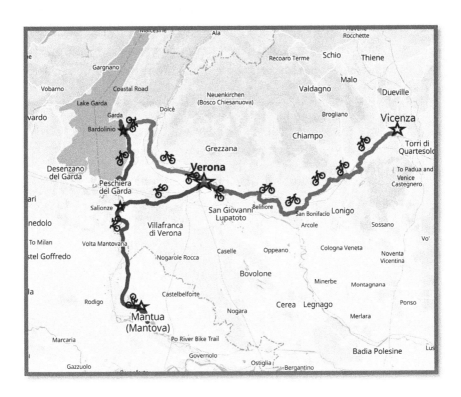

✝ Verona to Lake Garda

- The ride from Verona to the town of Garda, on Lake Garda, is 31 km, but involves mostly road riding and some hills. There are several roads that can be taken for this ride, so a round-trip can be accomplished using different routes.
- One route that includes more river riding is heading northwest out of Verona, toward Bussolengo, and continue to Rivoli. After Rivoli cross under the highway (14 km from Bussolengo), and head generally west to Bardolino following SP29c and SP32 (14km further). This route totals 42 km.
- Enjoy the resort towns of Bardolino and Garda, and Lake Garda -- a truly beautiful natural wonder.
- Ride back to Verona, or even better continue riding 18 km south on the lake to Peschiera del Garda and take a short train ride back. If you have more energy, consider riding 5 km further to the historic town of Sirmione, with much to see.

Lake Garda is a beautiful lake, formed by a glacier, with a maximum depth of 446 feet, and 158 km of shoreline.

The lake and shoreline are divided among three Italian provinces: Verona, Brescia, and Trento. The lake serves as a tourist mecca with beaching, sailing, kiteboarding, and resort fun.

There are many picturesque towns to visit and stay, including the ancient fortified city of Sirmione with the Grotte di Catullo and the 13th century Scaliger Castle.

✝ Around Lake Garda

- Lake Garda is the largest lake in Italy, and well worth a visit and even a stay (there are several bike riding-focused hotels near the lake for extended ride vacations).
- An extensive ferry system allows riders to explore the entire lake, and ride from one end to another and ferry back.
- Unless you want to include the ride over to the lake from Verona, as outlined above, consider a train to Peschiera del Garda, a quick 15-minute train ride, to launch your lake adventure.
- An extensive bike trail network is planned for Lake Garda, so check on developments before your ride. It is expected to have 140 km completed by 2021, but it appears delayed. Otherwise, riding is sometimes on roads and some trails with spectacular views, but often with some traffic and hills.
- Ride north to Bardolino and Garda (18 km). Enjoy these pleasant resort towns and beautiful views, and ride back to Peschiera for train back to Verona (36 km round-trip).
- Consider a 44-km further ride along the east side of the lake to Riva del Garda, and ferry back to Peschiera or Garda.
- Train back to Verona.

✝ Verona to Vicenza

- The Republic of Venice generally controlled the northeastern Italian region of Veneto, and there are some fantastic rides throughout this region. It is one of the flattest parts of Italy, which makes it one of my favorite riding areas!
- The 68-km ride from Verona to Vicenza is a good choice, though hilly and sometimes on small roads rather than on a bike path. The route takes riders through the Italian countryside and to the interesting city of Vicenza.
- Head west from Verona toward San Martino Buon Albergo, cross south of the A4 highway and head to Belfiore, San Bonifacio, Monteforte d'Alpone, Montebello Vicentino, Brendola, then traverse hills up and down to Vicenza.

- Plan a couple of hours to explore Vicenza, with the amazing architecture of Palladio, including the Palladian Basilica, the Palazzo Chiericati, the Teatro Olimpico, and the Villa La Rotonda.
- Take quick train back to Verona (under 40 minutes).

✝ Verona to Mantua (Mantova)

- This interesting 69-km ride connects Verona and Lake Garda with the historic city of Mantua, located on the Po River. The Po River also offers a great flat bike route connecting Milan to the Adriatic coast.
- Experience quiet flat river riding along the Mincio River route.
- Ride west from Verona to Salionze (25 km), which is on the Mincio River. Alternatively, take the train to Peschiera, explore the lake, then head south on the river.
- The ride from Peschiera to Mantua is 44 km, partially on a classic flat river trail, and the ride from Salionze is 7 km shorter. From Pozzolo Sul Mincio, heading south, the path moves away from the river and becomes a straight bike trail through quiet villages to Mantova.
- Explore the interesting city of Mantua, including museums and the Ducal Palace, adorned with frescoes by Andrea Mantegna.
- Train 50 minutes back to Verona.

Padua Rides

Padua is one of my favorite cities in Italy, but so few Americans actually plan a stay here. Visitors are understandably attracted to nearby Venice, Verona, and Florence, but Padua makes a welcome break from the crowds and a nice addition to a general Italian tour. Padua is home to a historic 13th century university that hosted many greats, including Galileo, and boasts one of the first botanic gardens. It also has an attractive historic old town with marvelous architecture, including a Jewish heritage quarter. A highlight is the Scrovegni Chapel, with its incredible Giotto frescoes that some consider the first major piece of modern art. There are many potential rides from Padua, but two are presented here: one to the architectural center of Vicenza, and the second to the charming town of Chioggia south of Venice on the lagoon. The Bikeline Vento map book, or a good local map or GPS, are recommended for these rides, since they are often not well-marked routes.

RIDE HIGHLIGHTS

+ Opportunity to ride in Italy without hills and mostly on bike trails or quiet roads -- unlike many areas in Italy that are quite hilly.

+ Great art, history, historic architecture, and Italian food!

+ **Getting There**: Train from Venice, Verona, Bologna, or Florence.

Padua to Vicenza Bike Route

Bike Path to Vicenza

RIDE FEATURES

🏨 Hotels:

- The Hotel Grand Italia is well-priced and located near the train station as well as walking distance to the sites. Good breakfast. Attractive value for room quality because not in center of historic area, but convenient especially if taking trains.

🚲 Bike Rental:

- Forever Bike (www.foreverbike.com).
- Mr. Bike (www.mr-bike.business.site).

RIDES

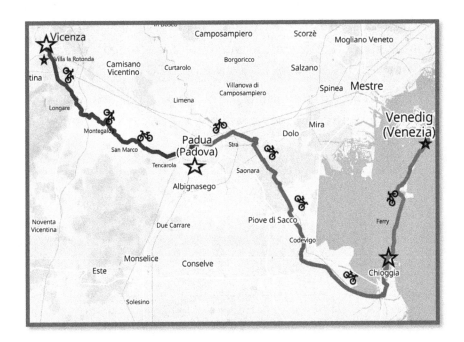

✝ Padua to Vicenza Ride.

- Consider a day ride to Vicenza (50 km), also mentioned as a ride destination from Verona.

- This is a pleasant ride (not all paved), generally flat, with a terrific gelato stop in Montegalda, and then a 30-minute train ride back to Padua.

- Head west from Padua toward Tencarola, and Pralungo, crossing the river near Creola Selvazzano, to San Marco, Montegalda, Ghizzole, and Longare, as you make your way to Vicenza.

- When approaching Vicenza look for Palladio's Villa la Rotonda on the distance on the left and consider a stop.

- Plan a couple of hours to explore Vicenza, with the amazing architecture of Palladio.

We really enjoyed exploring the Orto Botanico di Pradova, which is the formal name of Padua's botanical gardens. Founded in 1545, it is considered the world's oldest academic botanic garden still in operation and is now a UNESCO-designated site.

Visit exhibits outside, include the medicinal garden, as well as the extensive modern indoor facility with over 7,000 specimens featuring 3500 botanical species.

Andrea Palladio lived 1508-1580, and was one of the great Italian Renaissance architects, heavily influenced by classical Greek and Roman architecture.

He designed 23 projects in Vicenza, including the Palladian Basilica, the Palazzo Chiericati, the Teatro Olimpico (1555), and the Villa La Rotonda – as well as several projects in Venice.

His influence reached the United States, inspiring Thomas Jefferson for his Monticello as well at the U.S. Capitol building, and Congress once named him the "Father of American Architecture".

Venice

Beautiful Chioggia

✝ Padua to Chioggia Ride

- This 70-km ride is along bike paths and small roads, generally flat, to the attractive town of Chioggia, on the lagoon south of Venice, with its beaches and canals.
- This is a relatively more complicated route that is not well marked.
- Head out of Padua east to Stra, then toward Sandon, Codevigo, and then along a relatively straight route to Chioggia.
- It can be a bit tricky getting into Chioggia, some limited road riding.
- Take a 2-hour train back to Padua.
- Recommended: If you are fine with a long 95-km ride and get an early start from Padua, consider the fantastic ride continuing all the way to Lido from Chioggia (an additional 25 km further) with a combination of ferry rides along the barrier islands. Then from Lido take the Number 17 car ferry from Lido to the Venice train station, and a 30-minute train back to Padua.

Venice Rides

Venice is one of the great cities in the world, but not known for bike riding. Actually, visitors cannot bring their bikes into Venice any longer (I did 20 years ago, but no more), so the idea of bike riding as part of a Venice vacation is often not considered. However, bike riding is very possible if you stay in Lido, across the lagoon from central Venice, and purchase a ferry pass that can whisk you to all corners of the city and the lagoon, while having a refuge away from the crowds and a beach nearby. It is also possible to stay in Venice and rent a bike in Lido for day rides. I recommend a pair of day rides from Lido.

RIDE HIGHLIGHTS

+ Rides combine the magic of Venice with exploration of the surrounding area.

+ Explore the lagoon outside of Venice.

+ Beaches and small villages in the Vento.

+ **Getting There:** Take a ferry from the Venice train station or airport to Lido.

Car Ferry Connecting Lido and Venice Train Station   *Chioggia*

RIDE FEATURES

🏨 Hotels:

- Consider overnight in Lido at the historic Grand Albergo Ausonia and Hungaria Hotel, with its unusual facade. Good location and unique environment, with a Thai spa in the hotel that is great after a day of riding. Only a 5- minute walk to the ferry dock to Venice and surrounding areas.
- Hotel Giardinetto is also convenient, offering simple, small rooms. It is near the ferry as well.

🚲 Bike Rental:

- Venice Bike Rental (venicebikerental.bsuiness.site), which is actually located in Lido.
- Gardin Bicycle Rental and Sales (biciclettegardin.com).

RIDES

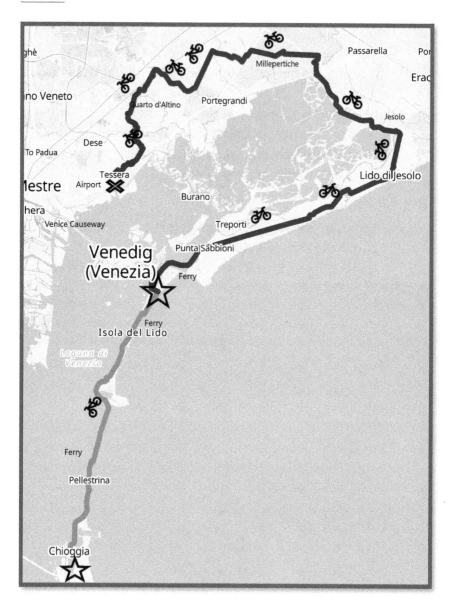

✝ Lido to Chioggia

- This is a beautiful easy ride (25 km each way) along the outer barrier islands, formed on the Adriatic side of the lagoon, and ending in Chioggia.
- Multiple ferries are involved, so purchase a multi-day boat pass, good for all the ferries and boats needed on this trip and in Venice.
- In Chioggia, enjoy a scrumptious lunch along a canal or seaside, and spend time exploring this delightful town and historic center. A great place to enjoy local beaches far from the crowds of Venice.
- Ride back to Venice (50-km round-trip).

Lido is a 11 km barrier island and home to over 20,000 residents. It might be most famous for hosting the Venice Film Festival in late August and early September. We were once in Lido during the festival – crowded, but much fun and exciting!

✝ Lido Loop Ride

- This is a 64 km loop north along the barrier islands and then back around the lagoon back to Venice, gives riders a sampling of the entire region.
- Head north on the barrier islands from Lido toward Jesolo. Once you depart from the barrier island route riding north from Lido the route can become a bit more complicated, sometimes riding on small roads as you make your way to various target towns on the route.
- The ride from Lido to Lido di Jesolo along the barrier islands is 25 km, using a ferry from Lido north.
- Ride inland to Jesolo, and follow the bike trail near the marshlands and river to Caposile, then Millepertiche (15 km). This avoids more traffic than along the Caposile to

Portegrandi road. Follow the route to Marteggia (under highway) to Bagaggiolo and then to Quarto d'Altino (12 km).

- At this point you can train 35 minutes back to Venice station and the ferry to Lido on the car ferry (52-km route).
- Otherwise, continue toward San Liberale and ride to the Venice International Airport (12 km). Take the train back to Venice train station for car ferry to Lido, or ferry from airport to Lido. Do check if they will accept bikes, since this policy changes. (total 64 km.)
- There is also the option to ride back to the Venice train station, although it involves riding across the not-bike friendly causeway. Not recommended.

Florence Rides

Florence is a wonderful city, offering good city riding and many rides around Tuscany. Rides tend to be hilly and on roads, less on bike trails, but sometimes on small quiet unpaved roads. This is not the typical river riding often highlighted in this book! Consider the two day rides described here to Siena and around the Chianti region. There are also day ride cycle tours offered from Florence-based companies; given the hills, this might also make an attractive choice.

RIDE HIGHLIGHTS

✦ Enjoy historic cities of Florence and Siena.

✦ Beautiful rides through the quiet heart of Tuscany in the Chianti region.

Florence   *Michelangelo's David*

163

RIDE FEATURES

▦ Hotels:

- Hotel Delgli Orafi is special, next to the Uffizi Gallery and with other major sites within 5-minute walk. Located on the river, it has a beautiful rooftop bar with views of the Duomo and the river. Very friendly, good breakfast in historic room.

🚲 Bike Rental:

- There are many bike rental locations in Florence, but consider Tuscany Cycle, with a variety of bike rentals, including nicer road bikes (www.tuscanycycle.com).
- Alinari Rental offers a variety of bikes for rent (www.alinairirental.com).
- Consider a bike tour with I Bike Tuscany (www.ibiketuscany.com). Given that the riding in Tuscany tends to be on roads, hilly, and not on bike trails, going with an all-inclusive day ride with this group, including bike and support, is a reasonable option to consider.

RIDES

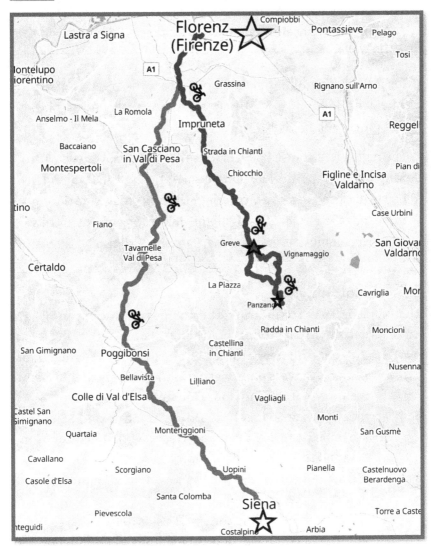

☦ Florence to Siena

- This 64-km ride looks quite interesting, but I have not undertaken it myself. It involves climbing and road riding, as is the case generally around Florence.
- Either ride the SR 222 toward Le Bolle, past Greve in Chianti, to Castellina in Chianti, to Fonterutoli, to the interesting city of Siena. Alternatively, follow smaller roads generally toward

San Casciano, Travarnelle, Poggibonsi, and Monteriggioni on the way to Siena.

- Enjoy Siena and train back to Florence (1.5 hours).

Chianti is a beautiful hilly area of Tuscany, between Florence and Siena. Rides take you through enchanting vineyards, olive tree groves and fields.

The region is of course known for its wine, generally made with Sangiovese grapes. While you often don't find the traditional bottle enclosed in a straw covering – having great wine during these rides is certainly a highlight! Interesting towns in this region including Greve, Castellina, Panzano, Radda, and Gaiole.

✝ Chianti Ride.

- This 85-km roundtrip ride combines road riding on SR 222, and small roads (often dirt) though the quieter Chianti areas.
- Ride out of Florence to SR 222, and head to Greve in Chianti (26 km). Greve is often viewed as the gateway to the Chianti region when coming from Florence.
- Ride south and then head to Vignamaggio and Lamole (5 km), the historic house that was the birthplace of Mona Lisa and near Leonardo's home as a youth.
- Ride small (often dirt) roads to Volpaia (13 km), a small medieval village.
- Head back west along the small roads to Panzano (10 km), which stands in the middle between Siena and Florence, and has been fought over for centuries. Check out the historic the bell tower of the church in the Panzano Alto.
- Ride back to Florence on SR 222 (31 km).
- Consider shorter rides through this area with organized companies, like I Bike Tuscany, which will shuttle you to the heart of the Chianti area, avoiding the longer rides in and out of Florence.

FRANCE

Cycling through France is a joy, especially near the Loire and Rhine Rivers, and along some of France's canal system bike routes. These rides offer beautiful countryside, historic chateaus and castles, interesting museums and attractions, fascinating historic towns, and, of course, incredible food! The French authorities have recognized the potential of the bike touring market, and have invested in improving the cycling infrastructure, trails, and signage, all of which make riding in France an even better cycling experience than ever before.

- **Blois** – Blois is located in the heart of the Loire Valley and a short train ride from Paris, making it an ideal base for exploring the famous chateaus and castles of the Loire Valley, including Chambord, Chaumont-Sur-Loire, and Cheverny.

- **Amboise** – Amboise is my favorite base city in the Loire River Valley, a great place from which to explore multiple chateaus, including Chenonceau, Villandry, Chaumont, Cheverny, and Chambord. Be sure to visit the Le Clos -- last home to Leonardo -- and stay in the fabulous Chateau de Prey Hotel.

- **Nantes** – Nantes is located in the heart of Brittany, a couple hours train ride from Paris, providing an opportunity to ride the Loire River far away from the classic chateau area. In this area of the Loire, be sure to visit the Brittany region, medieval towns, and at the end of the river trail as it reaches the Atlantic Ocean, the massive concrete German World War Two submarine base in St. Nazaire. Get a taste of canal riding as you explore the Nantes-Brest Canal unpaved pathway.

◉ Strasbourg – Strasbourg is an international city, combining a historic core and modern European government center, making it a good base for experiencing a Rhine River ride or a canal ride to the beautiful smaller town of Colmar.

◉ Colmar – Colmar is a charming, smaller historic town, with cobblestone streets and canals, and is the perfect base for day riding, including across the Rhine River to the university city of Freiburg in Germany or by canal trail to Strasbourg.

Blois Rides

The Loire River valley is one of my favorite regions for short day riding. Great historic sites, river bike trails, and fantastic food. Either Blois or Amboise make terrific towns for overnights, providing local attractions, nice hotels, good train logistics, and plenty of good eating! The rides suggested in both these chapters can be taken from either city with additional riding or train connections. For example, the ride from Blois to Chambord or Cheverny can be embarked upon from Amboise, albeit with a bit more riding, or involving a short train ride from Amboise to Blois to start the ride. Between the cities, I prefer staying in Amboise, but your decision might be based on which rides you want to enjoy and riding distances.

RIDE HIGHLIGHTS

✦ Classic chateau region, with wine, food, and castles.

✦ Amazing meals and pastries, of course.

✦ Stop at local wineries.

✦ Interesting historic hotels that were former chateaus.

✦ Good route signs for most rides.

✦ **Getting There:** Train from Paris (Montparnasse or Austerlitz) in under a two-hour train ride.

Blois from Bike Trail   *Ride to Chateau Chambord*

RIDE FEATURES

▥ Hotels:

- Consider the Mercure Blois Centre, the Best Western Blois Chateau, or the Ibis Blois Centre Chateau, all of which are well-located and can offer attractive pricing.

🚲 Bike Rental:

- Detours De Loire, offers a variety of bikes, including e-bikes (www.detourdeloire.com).

RIDES

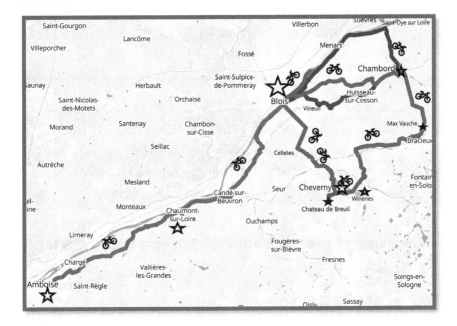

✝ Blois to Amboise Ride

- This 42-km ride from Blois to Amboise is worth the calories burned!
- Riding along the Loire River following the signs to Amboise. Cross the river at Blois, and head southwest along the Loire River.
- Pedal over a few small hills, following the route to Chaumont (20 km from Blois). Explore the Chateau de Chaumont.
- Continue another 22 km to Amboise, generally staying near the river and following the route signs.
- In Amboise enjoy great sites, including the castle and the Clos-Luce, with its fascinating Leonardo da Vinci exhibits. This was Leonardo's last home, with exhibits highlighting his many inventions.
- Take quick 15-minute train ride back to Blois.

✝ Blois to Chambord Ride

- This is 38-km round-trip ride is easy and beautiful, taking you along the Loire River to the Chateau de Chambord, arguably the grandest of all chateaus.

Chambord was constructed by Francis 1 (1519-1547). Plan to spend several hours exploring the grand Chateau and gardens. Most of the furnishings were sold or destroyed during the French Revolution, so the building interior can seem a bit barren. But the architecture and views from the roof are amazing.

Touring the gardens by bike is especially enjoyable, somewhat avoiding the crowds, which can average over 700,000 annually.

- There are two routes to Chambord, so make it a round-trip with use of both routes. Cross the river at Blois, head northeast along the Loire River on the bike trail (some is not paved) to Sant-Dye sur Loire. Explore this scenic village.
- Head away from the river almost due south at Saint-Dye to Chambord (total route of 21 km).
- On your return ride west from Chambord through a rural path, past Huisseau to Vineuil, and finally back to Blois on this 17-km route.

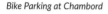

Bike Parking at Chambord   *Dogs after Feeding at Cheverny*

✝ Blois to Cheverny Direct Ride

- This ride is 15 km each way, crossing the river, and heading on the direct route southwest out toward Sant Gervais la Foret along the D765, and the D102 (about 4 km to Cheverny). There are longer routes with more scenic bike trails, as described in Grand Loop route below.
- Plan a couple of hours to visit the Chateau di Cheverny, its gardens, and the Tintin exhibit. Time your visit early enough to watch the dog feeding (usually 11:30 a.m.)!

✝ Grand Loop: Chambord, Cheverny, and More.

- This is a terrific full 74+-km day ride loop to two major chateaus and others along the way.
- Ride the 21-km or 17-km route to Chambord, as described in the Chambord ride, above. Enjoy Chambord.
- From Chambord ride south through parkland to Bracieux.

A great stop along this route is in Bracieux -- the award-winning Chocolaterie Max Vauche.

This wonderful shop and small chocolate factory was founded in 1999.

Best of all, plenty of free chocolate samples can be enjoyed by all! For a change of pace from the chateaus circuit, take a brief tour of the factory or participate in a workshop on making chocolate creations.

- Ride west, then follow signs heading south toward Cour-Cheverny and to the Chateau at Cheverny.
- As mentioned, plan a couple of hours to visit the Chateau de Cheverny, its gardens, dog feeding, and the Tintin exhibit.
- Take direct 15-km route back to Blois or continue along the bike route.
- If continuing on the bike route head southwest to Le Breuil. Recommended: consider a special meal at the hotel at the Chateau de Breuil, which also makes a special place for a premium stay and a good location for a couple of day rides from a country estate location near several vineyards.

Chateau de Brueil   Armor at Chateau de Prey Hotel

- Follow the route northwest to Cormeray to Cellettes. Just after Cellettes head due west for 1.6 km to a bike path taking riders back toward Blois avoiding the busy D956 road. Cross the river back to Blois.

Amboise Rides

Not to repeat what was just said about Blois, but this is a great place to base for riding around the wonderful Loire River Valley. Between staying at Blois and Amboise, I prefer Amboise, given the Chateau Royal D'Amboise on the river, the Son et Lumiere light show at night, and some of my favorite hotels, including the Chateau de Prey. I especially enjoy the Clos-Luce, with its fascinating Leonardo da Vinci exhibits. This was Leonardo's last home. The exhibits highlight his many inventions, with his drawings converted into models that demonstrate his genius. A terrific visit for all ages, with a garden and playground for children.

RIDE HIGHLIGHTS

+ Classic chateau region, with wine, food, and castles.

+ Amazing meals and pastries, of course.

+ Interesting historic hotels that were former chateaus.

+ Leonardo's last home and evening light show.

+ Chateau Royal d'Amboise.

+ **Getting There:** Train from Paris (Montparnasse or Austerlitz) for under two-hour train ride.

Chateau Royal d'Amboise   *Amboise*

175

RIDE FEATURES

🏨 Hotels:

- Consider a stay at the wonderful Chateau de Prey Hotel, one of my favorites (4 stays over 30 years), but also more expensive than my usual budget. Note that it is not in the center of town, but about 3 km out.
- If you prefer to stay in the center of town, consider the Hotel Pavilion Des Lys or other more moderately priced hotels.

The Chateau de Prey Hotel is something special. When else do you get a chance to stay in a hotel dating back to 1224, which has suits of armor from the original owners in the hallway and a nice pool?

The hotel also houses a Michelin 1-star restaurant, where we had the best meal of our trip, and easy walk back to the room after some wine!

My son and I spent almost an hour exploring the cheese cart with our patient guide, François. I didn't realize there was so much to learn about cheese!

The meal cost about $150 for both of us, the most expensive of our trip by a long shot, but it was also the most memorable meal of our years of riding together. Staying at a hotel like this gives riders the luxurious experience provided by higher-end tour companies -- but for a fraction of the price!

🚲 Bike Rental:

- Roue Lib offers a large variety of bike rentals, including e-bikes, tandems, child trailers, and traditional bikes. Multiple accessories available for rent, including bags and adult or child helmets (www.rouelib.eu).

RIDES

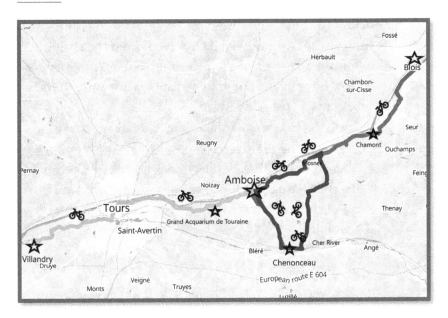

✝ Amboise to Blois Ride

- This 42-km ride from Amboise to Blois is the reverse of the ride offered out of Blois.
- Head out on the Loire River, following the signs to Blois, with a few small hills to the Chateau de Chaumont (22 km).
- Ride toward Chailles, and then to Blois (20 km).
- Cross over bridge to Blois.
- Explore this terrific town.
- Take a quick 15-minute train ride back to Amboise or make it a round-trip bike ride.

🗲 Amboise to Chenonceau Ride

- This 44-km loop to Chenonceau requires a bit of climbing as riders leave the Loire River and head to the Cher River where you will find the Chenonceau Chateau, probably my favorite chateau in the region.
- There is a direct short route to the Chateau, but the loop described herein takes riders northeast along the south side of the Loire River from Amboise to Mosnes and Rilly-sur-Loire. At Vesnon, head east away from the river, then follow the bike route southwest along route D27 to Vallieres-les-Grandes. Continue on the route, with some hills, to Chisseaux on the Cher River.
- A short distance west is the Chateau de Chenonceau.
- Continue along the river and past Civray de Touraine and take the route to la Chevroliere back northeast to Amboise along the bike path, which runs near route D81. After 8 km join D81 and ride along a road. The last stretch into Amboise is a bit hilly.

The Chateau de Chenonceau spans the River Cher, and is one of the most photographed sites in the Loire River tour. Dating as far back as the 11th century, the current chateau was built 1514-1522. This is a must stop on any Loire River tour.

Chateau du Close Luce and Leonardo Exhibit

Chateau de Villandry

✝ Amboise to Villandry Ride

- This ride is the opposite direction from Blois through Tours to Villandry (totaling 50 km).
- Head west out of Amboise toward Tours.
- Consider a stop at the Loire Aquarium, described in more detail below.
- Generally following the river or nearby route, arrive in Tours (28 km).
- Tours is a good lunch stop and take a quick look around in this larger town.
- Continue on a 22-km ride to the Chateau de Villandry. It can be a bit complicated leaving Tours, but follow the route signs. Cross the Cher River (Tours is sandwiched between the Loire River on the north, and the Cher River on the south). Follow the Cher River on the south side heading west to Les Vallees.
- Continue to Savonnieres and then Villandry.
- Visit the Chateau at Villandry, dating to 1536, but even better, the amazing world-class gardens.
- Ride back to Tours for 25-minute train ride back to Amboise, and total bike ride of 72 km. Note: there could be a train stop closer to Villandry, such as Berthenay, check with local stations.

Loire Aquarium

Bike Trail from Amboise

✝ Amboise Loire Aquarium Ride.

- Riding to the Aquarium de Touraine from Amboise is a good short day ride, especially with kids.
- Total ride is 8 kms each way and can be included on a ride to Tours.
- The aquarium has an interesting exhibit of the sea life in the Loire River as well as other ocean exhibits.

Nantes Rides

Nantes offers an interesting change from the classic Loire River Valley riding. Set in the heart of the Brittany region, Nantes has a different feel than other parts of France as well as a different history. A variety of day rides are available, including two rides along the Loire River and a ride on the Nantes-Brest Canal for a very different experience. Nantes also presents interesting sightseeing for times off the bike.

RIDE HIGHLIGHTS

✦ French Canal Riding! The Nantes-Brest Canal Ride.

✦ Two rides along the Loire, to the medieval city of Angers, or St. Nazaire, and the German Submarine World War Two base.

✦ **Getting There:** Train from Paris (two hours from Paris Montparnasse) or Amboise/Blois.

Fuel for the Ride

View of the Maine River from Angers Castle

181

RIDE FEATURES

⊞ Hotels:

- The Hotel Duquesne is well-priced, centrally located, and ideal for cycle touring.

🚲 Bike Rental:

- Bike'N Tour provides classic hybrid bikes (21 speeds), and e-bikes. A variety of bike tours also offered (www.bikentour.com).

RIDES

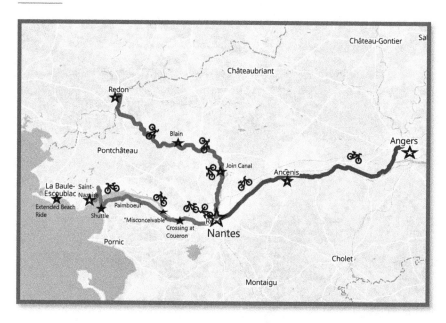

✝ Nantes to St. Nazaire

- This is an enjoyable 67-km ride to the mouth of the Loire River and St. Nazaire with its giant German World War Two submarine base remnants and exhibits. This is generally a well-marked route.
- Head out of Nantes on the north side of the river. Consider a highly recommended stop to see the Machines of the Isle of Nantes.

One of the most unexpected sites of all my rides was when we came upon a mechanical elephant the size of a small house walking not far from the bike path out of Nantes on the Ile De Nantes. We were invited to climb in for a ride in what looked like a high-tech form of a Trojan Horse!

In addition to the giant elephant, there was much more to see in this fascinating complex, including the Machine Gallery. Great for all ages, especially families. There is also a potential stop at the nearby Jules Verne Museum, opened in 1978, to mark the 150th anniversary of Verne's birth in Nantes.

- Further along the trail cross to the south side of the Loire River. There are two places to cross by ferry: Indre or further along at Coueron.
- At Indre, ride 1 km inland and rejoin the Loire trail ride with good signage.
- A good stop is at Pellerin, across the river from Coueron. One of the best pastries and bread shops on the ride!
- Just west of the town, stop at the incredible drooping sailboat sculpture at the Ile De Bois, "Misconceivable."

"Misconceivable" is a sculpture created in 2007, by the Austrian artist Erwin Wurm, also called the "soft boat." Mr. Wurm built his creation by transforming an old boat and other real boat parts.

183

- Visit the tourist office at Paimboeuf and consider a walking tour.
- There is a new bike trail from Paimboeuf along the river to the large bridge that crosses to the north side of the Loire River.
- THE BRIDGE -- I rode over this 3.5 km bridge once and am still having nightmares! People do walk on the narrow sidewalk along the bridge, but not recommended. Given how bad this ride is, the local authorities have organized a free shuttle service for bikes and riders, leaving 9 times a day until 7:00 p.m., just past the bridge in St. Brevin near the serpent sculpture on the beach. Much appreciated, but no tandems! If you miss this shuttle, also look for Bus #17, which can take bikes across.
- In St. Nazaire visit the historic German Submarine base and learn about the history of the U-boats.
- Take a 35-minute train ride back to Nantes.
- For more riding continue toward La Baule-Escoublac, and enjoy this beach resort, and then take a 50-minute train ride back to Nantes.

St. Nazaire Bridge Over the Loire River
- Take the Shuttle! -

Redon on the Brest-Nantes Canal

✝ Nantes to Ancenis/Angers

- There are two options for this ride: ride along the Loire River east to Ancenis (38 km) or if looking for something longer, ride further to Angers (88 km total). These are generally well-marked routes.
- Head east out of Nantes on the north side of the Loire River trail to Mauves, and then cross the river. Follow the river trail on the south side, crossing at Oudon, where you can visit the castle and small town.
- Continue on the north side of the river to Ancenis and take some time to explore the city. Take a 20-minute train ride back to Nantes or continue to Angers.
- Take the train back from Angers (about a 40-minute ride).

✝ Taste of the Nantes-Brest Canal Ride

- Riding along the Nantes-Brest Canal is a pleasure, but it is not an easy day ride. First, you need to get there. This involves a 26-km ride to the beginning of the canal trail. Next, there are no trains back (that I have identified) until Redon, which is another 100km, making for a very long day. There are buses back from various cities but do confirm they accept bikes before planning on using them.
- The canal was built in the early 19th century, running 360 km with 238 locks, connecting the seaports of Nantes and Brest in Brittany.
- There is no towpath on the canal out of Nantes, so head 26 km along a somewhat hilly road route to lock Number Two, where you will begin the ride. Take the D39 and then D69 toward La Chappelle-sur-Erdre and Suce-sur-Erdre, turning toward the canal before the junction between D69 and D26.
- Join the flat, mostly packed surface ride along the canal towpath. Visit the mechanical locks operated by staff at lock houses. Watch rented holiday boats glide by.
- Continue 50 km to Blain. Check for bus schedules back if this is your finishing point for the day.

- One option is to spend the night in Blain, carrying only one set of off-bike clothing and necessities, and then continuing to Redon the next day.
- Continue to Redon (another 50 km). Redon is an interesting inland port city with a large church, Abbey, and old streets. Consider a meal at the Creperie l'Akene.
- Enjoy a one-hour train ride back to Nantes.

For a change of pace, consider renting a houseboat for a cruise-cycling adventure along the Nantes-Brest Canal. What a wonderful way to unpack for a stay in one space, and explore the canal with day rides.

Boats range from 9 to 15 meters — and no license needed! We saw many of these boats as we pedaled along the pathway.

Strasbourg Rides

Strasbourg serves as a fantastic base, with its interesting sites, neighborhoods, and restaurants that extend from the historic city to the modern EU government headquarters area. Ride on a French canal to Colmar, cross the Rhine River to the German university town of Freiburg, or ride north along Rhine River and experience this mighty water highway. Consider combining these day rides with an additional stay in one of the nearby other base cities such as Stuttgart, Trier, or Heidelberg.

RIDE HIGHLIGHTS

✦ Rhine River and historic canal riding opportunities.

✦ Visit France and Germany.

✦ Generally good rail system.

✦ Amazing destinations including Colmar and Freiburg.

✦ **Getting There:** Train from Paris, Frankfurt, Stuttgart, or Zurich.

View From Stasbourg Cathedral Spire   *Vibrant Rhine River*

RIDE FEATURES

▦ Hotels:
- Consider the three-star Hotel Cathedrale, which is well-priced and with a great location in the center of town (www.hotel-cathedral.fr).

🚲 Bike Rental:
- Velhop bikes, which offers rather heavy bikes, but also e-bike options, child bikes, and tandems (www.velhop.stasbourg.eu). Five shops around town, so this is a convenient option.

RIDES

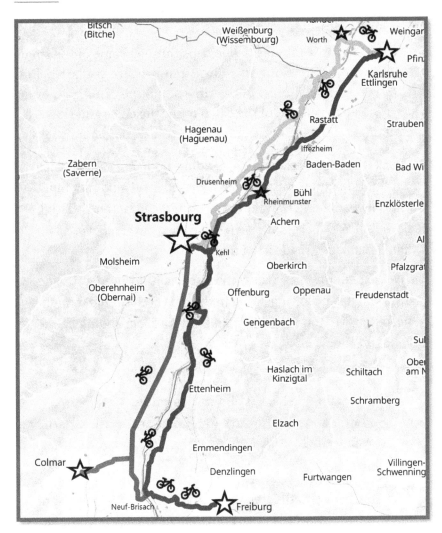

⳨ Strasbourg to Colmar Ride

- Ride to Colmar along the Canal Du Rhone au Rhine (75.5 km), which starts just southwest of the main hospital near Rue Humann. If you ever wanted to ride one of the canals of France, this is a great opportunity!

- Once on the canal trail (make sure you are on the right one given that several routes exist), head straight with one turn to Colmar.
- There are options for side trips through some of the small wine towns along this route, but because you are below ground level most of the time along the canal, you often need to ride out of the canal to see the cities and sites.

Check the wind direction before riding along the canal. I once did this ride myself entirely into a wicked headwind (not fun!). The only way I survived was putting on my headsets and blasting Bowie's *Let's Dance* album – which I played over and over again until I thankfully made it to Colmar!

That experience has made me especially focused on wind direction if it is blowing -- and in the case of this route it might make sense to train to Colmar and ride back depending on the wind direction.

- The train ride back is about 35 minutes.
- Plan a couple of hours for lunch and walking around wonderful historic Colmar.

The Strasbourg Cathedral dates back to 1439 – but more interestingly, it was the tallest building in the world from 1647 to 1874, with a spire reaching 142 meters. If you have time climb the seemingly never ending 330 steps up the spiral staircase to a panorama platform above the city – fantastic view!

✝ Strasbourg to Freiburg (Germany)

- This is an attractive ride, but longer (96 km), and with unpaved stretches and some hills the last stretch toward Freiburg -- making it a somewhat more challenging route than average for this book.
- There are routes on both sides of the Rhine River. On the west side riding is often along a canal pathway and then small roads before crossing the Rhine River, while on the east side riders cross the Rhine River near Strasbourg and then generally follow the river pathway with easy navigation, but often not on paved bike path.
- On the east side, ride Strasbourg to Rheinhausen along the river pathway (50 km) with no easy train connections back to Strasbourg. Bike 5 km further east to Herbolzheim for 1.1-hour train back if shorter ride sought. Continue along the river trail to Breisach and then ride over to Freiburg. There is also the option to leave the river earlier at Sasbach and head to Freiburg by small road.
- On the west side of the Rhine River, head from Strasbourg toward Eschau along the Rhine Canal pathway (same way as to Colmar), and then toward Artzenheim and Kunheim, then crossing the Rhine River near Neuf-Brisach to Breisach. Ride to Freiburg on smaller roads with some hills.
- Breisach is worth exploring, and after 80 km of riding, consider a train back to Strasbourg, about 40-minute trip.
- Breisach to Freiburg (an additional 16 km) on a more complicated path east of the Rhine River, with some hills.
- Plan a couple of hours to visit the beautiful university town of Freiburg.
- Take a 1.5-hour train ride back to Strasbourg.

✝ Strasbourg Rhine River Ride

- This ride heads north generally along the Rhine River, with a long ride to Karlsruhe, across the Rhine River (80 km total) but with shorter options available. There are cycle options on both sides of the Rhine.
- West -North Side of Rhine Route:
  - Strasbourg to Drusenheim along northwest side of Rhine (34 km), with a section cycling along a road from La Wantzenau past Gambsheim, to Herrlisheim, and then bike lane to Drusenheim. Note: there are not great train connections back to Strasbourg along this side of the river, so check with the local train station before leaving if planning on a shorter ride. However, there is a ferry crossing near Drusenheim, then short ride to Rheinmunster, and then return to Strasbourg with a 1.5-hour train ride back.
  - If going all the way to Karlsruhe, follow the Rhine River path to near Worth, then cross river into Karlsruhe.
- West-South Side of the Rhine Route:
  - Cross the Rhine River to Kehl, and then head north along the river trail (some parts of this path are not paved) toward Freistett.
  - Stay along the river route. Be aware that a few areas of this section are not paved.
  - Continue to Iffezheim. Another 35 km takes you to Karlsruhe, or opt for a short ride to Rastatt (about 45 km) and train back.
  - Visit the fabulous Kalrsruhe Place.
  - Train ride for return trip (1.2 hours).
  - For the Loop Route Option: consider riding on the west side of Rhine River to Drusenheim, take the ferry crossing, and then ride back on the east side of Rhine (about 69 km). **Important:** confirm the ferry is operating before embarking on this loop.

Colmar Rides

Colmar, located in France's Alsace region, is one of the special small towns that serves as a great base for multiple days of riding. The town can be quite crowded during the day with tour buses, but ride during the day and enjoy a quieter town in the late afternoons and evenings, when are you also free to indulge in one of the many local wines. Have fun strolling by the many canals and medieval half-timbered buildings. There are some overlaps to the rides provided for from Strasbourg, but Colmar presents a smaller, quainter, setting than Strasbourg. Ride a French canal to Strasbourg, or ride across the Rhine River to Freiburg and visit this historic university town.

RIDE HIGHLIGHTS

+ Rhine River and canal riding opportunities.

+ Visit France and Germany.

+ Generally good rail system.

+ Heart of a beautiful wine area.

+ Amazing destinations including Strasbourg and Freiburg.

+ **Getting There:** Train from Strasbourg, Paris, Frankfurt, Switzerland, or Stuttgart.

Beautiful City of Colmar

RIDE FEATURES

⌗ Hotels:

- Consider the Hotel Le Rapp, a fine 3-star hotel located near the old town and train station that includes a small indoor pool.

🚲 Bike Rental:

- Colmar Velo - Velodocteurs, with a variety of bikes (www.velodocteurs.com).
- Lulu Cycles, with a nice selection of bike types (www.lulucycles.com).

RIDES

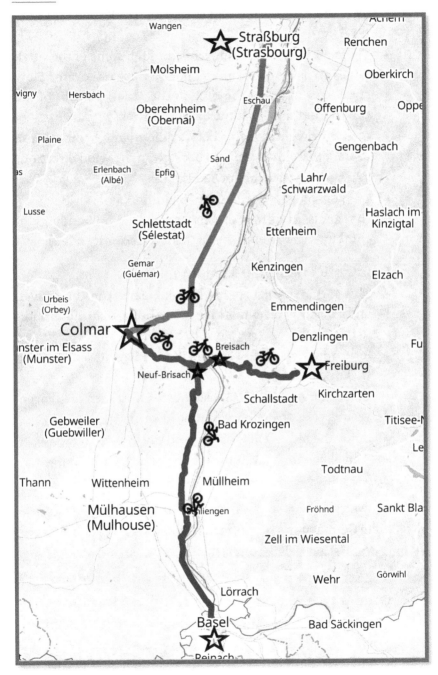

195

✝ Colmar to Strasbourg Ride

- Ride to Strasbourg along the Canal Du Rhone au Rhine (75.5 km).
- There are options for side trips through some of the small wine towns along the route, but because riders are below street level most of the time in the canal, ride out of the canals from time-to-time to visit the nearby villages.
- Check the wind direction before riding, it might make sense to train to Colmar and ride back given the wind direction.
- Train return takes about 35 minutes.
- Enjoy exploring Strasbourg, including a boat ride along the canals, a bus tour of the European Union buildings, or climbing the tower of the Cathedral (recommended).

✝ Colmar to Freiburg (Germany)

- This 45-km ride cuts perpendicular across the Rhine River, and as such involves more non-river riding than most routes in this book -- and, as a result, more hills.
- Ride from Colmar toward the Rhine River at Neuf-Brisach (17 km).
- Cross the river along D415, heading to Hochstetten, Merdingen, Weingarten, to Freiburg (about 16 km).
- Enjoy the old city of Freiburg and the university.
- Plan ahead for a 1.5-hour train ride back, with changes.

The University of Freiburg was founded in 1457, and is the fifth oldest in Germany. It is known for its humanities, social sciences and natural science departments.

✝ Colmar to Basel (Switzerland) Rhine River Ride

- Ride from Colmar toward the Rhine River at Neuf-Brisach (17 km).
- Proceed south down the Rhine River to Basel (59 km).
- Explore Basel. Train back (about one hour on the right trains).

CONCLUSION

The day rides recommended in this book give riders and visitors to Europe a chance to experience some of the best European bike rides without the time investment or hassles of a dedicated cycle touring trip (which I also love!).

This book provides opportunities to combine many base towns and routes and creatively fashion a trip that best meets your interests and schedule.

If you like what you find – there is always next year for a solid week or two of point-to-point cycle touring!

Enjoy, and be safe!

APPENDIX

Trip Checklist

- ☐ Select base city or cities.
- ☐ Reserve a hotel that meets your needs, interest, and budget.
- ☐ Reserve bikes ahead if possible. Decide on bike type (road, mountain, hybrid, e-bike) but sometimes the choices will be limited.
- ☐ Look for detailed maps, like the *Bikeline Guide* cycle map series, though often a simple area road map is all you need with these generally well-marked trails.
- ☐ Pack at least one set of riding cloths.
- ☐ Consider bringing your own helmet, day bags, and pedals -- or use the ones from the bike rental shop.
- ☐ Bring your cycling GPS if you have one.
- ☐ Complete a bit of riding at home to get ready if you have time.
- ☐ Prepare for some fun and adventure!

NOTES

ABOUT THE AUTHOR

Mike Lyon has been cycling for over 50 years, and has been touring in Europe through self-guided biking trips since 1994 -- the last eight years with his son Joshua on their tandem. He has also traveled extensively around-the-world, having visited over 100 countries for both work and pleasure.

When not cycling, Mike provides legal and international business development support to companies in the technology areas, with a focus on the space sector. Mike is a leader in space tourism, where he worked extensively on organizing the flights of space tourists who visited the International Space Station aboard Russian Soyuz spacecraft.

Mike also served in senior posts in the U.S. government, including as the Special Assistant to L. William Seidman at the Federal Deposit Insurance Corporation and Resolution Trust Corporation (U.S. Government Agencies) during America's Savings & Loan financial crisis.

Mike grew up riding in Evanston, Illinois, and received his J.D. from the Harvard Law School, and his B.A. in History from Brandeis University. He also attended the London School of Economics.

Mike lives and cycles in the Washington, D.C. area, with his wife, Kusavadee, and son, Joshua – his great cycling companion.

Mike Along the Elbe River

Mike and Joshua At Lake Garda

CPSIA information can be obtained
at www.ICGtesting.com
Printed in the USA
LVHW041327050622
720536LV00009B/743

9 780578 740546